The Heart of
Catholic Prayer

Rediscovering
the Our Father
and the
Hail Mary

MARK P. SHEA

Our Sunday Visitor Publishing Division
Our Sunday Visitor, Inc.
Huntington, Indiana 46750

Nihil Obstat
Msgr. Michael Heintz, Ph.D.
Censor Librorum

Imprimatur
✠ Kevin C. Rhoades
Bishop of Fort Wayne-South Bend
February 21, 2012

The *Nihil Obstat* and *Imprimatur* are official declarations that a book is free from
doctrinal or moral error. It is not implied that those who have granted the *Nihil Obstat*
and *Imprimatur* agree with the contents, opinions, or statements expressed.

The Heart of
Catholic Prayer

To my sweet love, Janet, who incarnates the love
of Christ and his Mother every day.

⁓

And to my Mother in Christ, the Blessed Virgin Mary:
Totus Tuus.

CONTENTS

Acknowledgments 9

Introduction: The Our Father and the Hail Mary 11

PART ONE: THE OUR FATHER

1. Our Father 19
2. Who Art in Heaven 25
3. Hallowed Be Thy Name 31
4. Thy Kingdom Come 35
5. Thy Will Be Done 45
6. On Earth as It Is in Heaven 53
7. Give Us This Day Our Daily Bread 61
8. And Forgive Us Our Trespasses . . . 69
9. And Lead Us Not Into Temptation 79
10. But Deliver Us from Evil 87

PART TWO: THE HAIL MARY

11. Hail Mary 103
12. Full of Grace 107
13. The Lord Is With Thee 111
14. Blessed Art Thou Among Women 117
15. And Blessed Is the Fruit of Thy Womb, Jesus 121
16. Holy Mary, Mother of God 131
17. Pray for Us Sinners 135
18. Now and at the Hour of Our Death 143

Afterword: Two Hearts in One 147
Notes 153
Selected Bibliography 157
About the Author 159

ACKNOWLEDGMENTS

Thanks, above all, to God — the Father, the Son, and the Holy Spirit — from whom, to whom, and through whom this book and all things exist. Blessed be he!

Thanks also to my wife, Janet, for showing me both Mary and Jesus in the beauty of her being, and to our kids: Luke, Tasha, granddaughter Lucy the Cuteness, Matthew, Claire, Peter, and Sean. I love you all and am so proud of you!

In addition, heaps o' thanks go to:

- Bert Ghezzi, Woodeene Koenig-Bricker, and all the good people at Our Sunday Visitor.
- The good folks who read my blog, *Catholic and Enjoying It!*
- Dave and Sherry Curp and all the Curplings.
- My dear friend Sherry Weddell and the gang at the Catherine of Siena Institute in Colorado Springs, Colorado. You guys do awesome work!
- Dale Ahlquist, president of the G. K. Chesterton Society, for being such a thoughtful and funny guy — like Chesterton, only thinner.
- G. K. Chesterton, who is not just Dale's hero but mine as well.
- C. S. Lewis, yet another of my heroes.
- J. S. Bach, The Montreux Band, Darol Anger, Mike Marshall, Pat Metheny, Phil Keaggy Nightnoise, Duke Ellington, They Might Be Giants: musicians whose beauty helped me write.
- The people of Blessed Sacrament Parish in Seattle, Washington. Thanks for being our home until we reach our Long Home.

- Also special thanks to Sts. Jerome, Athanasius, Anthony of the Desert, Francis de Sales, Dominic, Tertius — and of course, Mama Mary, on whose constant intercession I rely for help. *Ora pro nobis.*

The Our Father and the Hail Mary

Author Simon Tugwell, O.P., notes that, according to St. Paul, the very first thing we should know about prayer is that we do not know how to do it. Paul makes this fact clear when he tells the Romans that

> . . . the Spirit helps us in our weakness; for we do not know how to pray as we ought, but the Spirit himself intercedes for us with sighs too deep for words. And he who searches the hearts of men knows what is the mind of the Spirit, because the Spirit intercedes for the saints according to the will of God. (Romans 8:26-27)

Because we don't know what we are doing when we pray, God sends us help. The principal help he gives is the Spirit, who, if you will, prays through us and in union with us. That doesn't mean we are empty vessels and that every prayer that pops into our head is an oracular utterance of the very mind of God. It means that God the Holy Spirit guides and helps us to pray more and more like Christ in the power of his Sonship. That, in turn, directs us back to the fact that Christ is our teacher in the school of prayer, especially in and through his inspired word in Scripture and in the liturgy of the Church, since the Mass is the highest form of prayer. With his disciples, we say, "Lord, teach us to pray!" — and he does.

When we turn to Christ's teaching on prayer and the fact of the liturgy, we discover something odd: one of the many curiosities of the Christian tradition is that when Jesus undertakes to teach about prayer, he begins by waving us all away from meaningless repetitive prayer: "And in praying do not heap up empty phrases as the Gentiles do; for they think that they will be heard for their many words" (Matthew 6:7). But in the next breath, he gives us a prayer that he obviously expects us to repeat, a prayer we have indeed repeated for almost two thousand years — the Our Father. Is this a contradiction?

No. Jesus is warning against meaning*less* repetition, not meaning*ful* repetition. In this warning, he has in view a sort of magical notion of prayer, in which we can somehow gain power over the unseen by mere repetition or by saying just the right incantation so that God has to knuckle under to our will, like a genie. It reduces God to something like a capricious sprite who spends his days scrutinizing trivialities ("Was that ten Hail Marys you said this decade or only *nine*? Denied!"), rather than a God who is Father and filled with love for his children. There's something at once childlike, superstitious, and savage in such a picture of prayer, but you'd be surprised how easy it is to fall into.*

The same spirit which half-believes that if we step on a crack we'll break our mother's back constructs superstitious prayer practices that promise us "discipline" by laying out arbitrary rules and expecting them to save us. Such law-based notions of salvation deliver instead captivity to scruples and a vision of God as a kind of cosmic vending machine demanding correct change.

Against all such temptations to reduce God to a sort of faceless inscrutability awaiting the precisely spoken magic spell to subdue his power to our will, Jesus urges us in exactly the opposite direction: toward personal relationship. He wants childlike disciples, not childish ones. He makes this plain when he tells us to avoid the ways of the pagans, "for your Father knows what you need before you ask him" (Matthew 6:8).

---

* Curiously, it is children who are most likely to fall into this way of praying because they are the ones who really want what the English author Evelyn Waugh referred to as "little systems of order."

That's an odd thing to say if you think like a Greek logician. After all, if the Ground of Being knows what you need before you ask him, then why ask? But Jesus' logic is different. For Jesus, it is precisely because God knows us already that you can tell him anything. In short, it's all about a personal relationship. Prayer is not addressed to a God who has faded into a faceless, inscrutable Power. It is addressed to a thunderbolt who has revealed to us a Father's face. That is why the prayer begins "Our Father" and not "Master of the Universe." When he gives his disciples the model prayer, this is where he begins — with the fundamental fact of God as *Father*.

This shows us that the Our Father (also known as the Lord's Prayer) is a deeply *covenantal* prayer. But in our legalist culture of contracts, we don't especially think in terms of "covenant" these days. So until we understand what a covenant is, we are ill equipped to understand what the Our Father — much less the "new and eternal covenant" — is all about.[1]

In brief, a covenant is a bond of sacred kinship. Participants in a covenant become family. It differs from a contract in that it is not fifty-fifty, but hundred-hundred. In a contract, if I don't pay the gas station their hundred bucks, they don't owe me the tank of gas. If they don't pony up the gas, I don't owe them the hundred bucks. In a covenant, both parties pledge themselves to one another as family, and even if one does not honor the covenant, the other remains family. That does not mean people are free to abuse covenants, for a covenant always involves an oath, the Latin word for which is *sacramentum*, and the oath always involves blessings for keeping the covenant and curses for breaking it. (See the blessings and curses attending the Sinai covenant in Leviticus 26.) In the Christian tradition, the blessings and curses involve nothing less than heaven and hell.

There have been a series of covenants in salvation history involving Adam, Noah, Abraham, Moses, David, and finally, Jesus Christ. Divine covenants in Scripture are always mediated through some human agent who becomes a sort of father figure to the recipients of the covenant. In addition, the successive covenants build on one another (as we shall see, for instance, in the case of the relationship between Adam, David, and Jesus in Chapter 4). But all the covenants of the Old Testament are, in one way or another, incomplete without, and looking forward to, the new and everlasting covenant made through Jesus Christ and his passion, death, and resurrection. That is what he means when he tells us that he is the fulfillment of the law and the prophets (Luke 24:44).

In our baptism, we become family with God and he with us — adopted sons and daughters who are children of God in Christ. Our foundational relationship in such a covenant is not merely to God as Creator or Lawgiver or Master, but as Father. And so the entire tradition of Christian prayer begins with the words, "When you pray, say, 'Father . . .' " (Luke 11:2).

But this is not where Tradition ends, for Jesus doesn't just give us God as our Father. He also gives us Mary as our Mother with the words "Behold, your mother" (John 19:27). And so, it's no coincidence that the Our Father and the Hail Mary are closely intertwined in the heart of the Church. For instance, medieval rosaries were called "paternosters" ("Our Fathers"), and by the twelfth century the practice of reciting the Our Father on the beads had given way to reciting 50 or 150 "Ave Marias" ("Hail Marys"). A biographer of St. Albert the Great, the man who taught St. Thomas Aquinas, tells us, "A hundred times a day he bent his knees, and fifty times he prostrated himself, raising his body again by his fingers and toes, while he repeated at every genuflection: 'Hail Mary, full of grace, the Lord is with thee, blessed art thou amongst women and blessed is the fruit of thy womb.' "[2]

Five things are worth noting about this passage. First, despite today's Protestant jitters about the practice, the popular move toward asking Mary's intercession was not a "replacement" of God with Mary, for the Mass, the actual act of worship in the Catholic tradition, remained fixed and focused on the worship of the Blessed Trinity. Second, the fact that the prayer was recorded by the biographer (and not simply called the "Hail Mary") suggests that it was not yet well known in Albert's day. Third, this was the *whole* of the Hail Mary in Albert's day. Fourth, the second part of the prayer ("Holy Mary, Mother of God, pray for us sinners, now and at the hour of our death") did not stand as it does now until roughly the sixteenth century. Fifth, all of this points quite clearly to the fact that the Hail Mary is something that developed out of the hearts and minds of Christians meditating on the life of Jesus' greatest disciple, as it was revealed in Scripture and in the Tradition of the Church.

This is fitting, because the Hail Mary is profoundly the prayer of a *disciple*. Like the Rosary of which it forms such a vital part, it is a prayer ordered toward looking at Jesus through the magnifying lens of Mary's life. But it is also a prayer that teaches us to see Mary as the greatest recipient of grace, as well as our model and Mother in how to live out that life of grace in our day-to-day walk with Christ. It is a prayer that strings together the basic biblical teachings about Mary and quotes freely from (1) Luke's infancy narrative; (2) the Council of Ephesus, which declared Mary to be the "Mother of God"; and (3) the cry of the Catholic heart that she stand by our cross of death as she stood by Christ's.

Mary is the disciple who sticks with us in our wretchedness when all others have forsaken us, just as she stuck with Jesus. What the Hail Mary is *not* is a prayer that Mary take the place of God. The whole point about her is not that she is a goddess who stoops down to us and "empties herself" as Jesus did, but rather that she, being a mere mortal, is exalted by the grace of God to sit in the heavenlies with the Son of God.

In all this, Mary mirrors the faithfulness of God to us and teaches us to mirror that faithfulness to God and our neighbor. There is a profound sanity in this, which is exactly the sanity of the Gospel — the sanity of love. The whole nature of covenant is that it is about *family*. God has not willed to save us by ourselves alone but to save us through the mediation of our fellow human beings, with the Son of Man as chief Mediator and his Mother as the Mediatrix of All Grace. How can we address her by this audacious title? Because her Son *is* all grace, and it is through her freely given yes that God chose to send his Son into the world.

In the same way, we are made cooperators and co-laborers with Christ and become mediators of grace to our neighbor. Our relationship with God in Christ necessarily involves us in a relationship with his Body, the Church, of whom Mary is Mother, since she is the mother of "the rest of her offspring, . . . those who keep the commandments of God and bear testimony to Jesus" (Revelation 12:17). God has chosen to reveal himself, not via a direct encounter with his unveiled glory that would blast us to atoms (Exodus 33:22), but in a human way, through human things like bread, wine, and water, and via the human touch of a brother, a sister, a father — and a Mother. Mary stands as the great sign of this sacramental truth by being, as St. Ambrose reminded us, the type of the Church.[3] When we see Mary, we see an icon of the entire Church, perfected in the image of Christ, docile to his will, mighty with his power, gentle with his love, terrible as an army with banners. If we seek to be perfect disciples, we must look to the saints in whom the Spirit dwells, just as Paul told us to do when he said, "Be imitators of me, as I am of Christ" (1 Corinthians 11:1). The greatest disciple of them all is Mary, whose soul magnifies the Lord and (like all magnifiers) makes it easier for us to see him.

The Tradition of the Church has given such prominence to these two prayers because they are so profoundly expressive of the Church's heart and soul. To learn and understand the Our Father and the Hail Mary is to learn the deepest contours of the Church's interior life, for both are prayers that come from the Holy Spirit, who is the soul of the Church. Understanding this, let us then turn to these two jewels of the Church's deep tradition of prayer and hold them up to the light in order to see their facets, asking the Holy Spirit to draw us more deeply into the heart of the mystery of God's love for us.

PART ONE

THE OUR FATHER

Πάτερ ἡμῶν ὁ ἐν τοῖς οὐρανοῖς
ἁγιασθήτω τὸ ὄνομά σου
ἐλθέτω ἡ βασιλεία σου
γενηθήτω τὸ θέλημά σου,
ὡς ἐν οὐρανῷ καὶ ἐπὶ τῆς γῆς
τὸν ἄρτον ἡμῶν τὸν ἐπιούσιον δὸς ἡμῖν σήμερον
καὶ ἄφες ἡμῖν τὰ ὀφελήματα ἡμῶν,
ὡς καὶ ἡμεῖς ἀφίεμεν τοῖς ὀφειλέταις ἡμῶν
καὶ μὴ εἰσενέγκῃς ἡμᾶς εἰς πειρασμόν,
ἀλλὰ ῥῦσαι ἡμᾶς ἀπὸ τοῦ πονηροῦ.

Pater noster, qui es in caelis:
sanctificetur nomen tuum.
Adveniat regnum tuum.
Fiat voluntas tua,
sicut in caelo, et in terra.
Panem nostrum cotidianum da nobis hodie,
et dimitte nobis debita nostra,
sicut et nos dimittimus debitoribus nostris,
et ne nos inducas in tentationem,
sed libera nos a malo.

Our Father who art in heaven,
hallowed be thy name.
Thy kingdom come.
Thy will be done
on earth, as it is in heaven.
Give us this day our daily bread,
and forgive us our trespasses,
as we forgive those who trespass against us,
and lead us not into temptation,
but deliver us from evil.

Chapter 1

OUR FATHER

In Luke's Gospel, the Our Father, like so much else in Jesus' teaching, is occasioned by a request from his disciples: "Lord, teach us to pray, as John taught his disciples" (Luke 11:1). This should get our attention, because as is typical of Jesus' method of revelation, instead of going around, announcing, "Hey! I'm the Messiah!" he appears to leave so much to the initiative of others. Half of his sayings are replies and rejoinders to things somebody else said or asked. Even the great and shocking revelation of his identity as the Christ, the Son of the living God, is made, not by him directly, but *through* the apostle Peter. The disciple makes the great confession, "You are the Christ, the Son of the living God." Jesus then confirms it by telling Peter that flesh and blood has not revealed it to him, but "my Father who is in heaven" (Matthew 16:16-17). In both cases — the revelation of the Our Father and the Messianic revelation — had the disciples not made the request for instruction on prayer or plucked up the courage to make the shocking confession, we might never have received the revelation. That should stagger us, because it points to the first thing we should realize about prayer: the fact that we pray at all.

Of course, psychologically, prayer is perfectly understandable. There's no big shock about weak flesh crying out to the heavens for some sort of help in making it through this vale of tears. If we were all pagans, there would be no great surprise in the idea of our trying to wheedle and cajole the various clashing egos and agendas of the Olympians into playing favorites with us or scheming against other gods and humans in order to obtain some desired outcome to our plight.

But Christians do not believe in such a deity. We believe in a God who is omnipotent, all-knowing, and all-loving. That raises a huge question — namely, what's the point of prayer to such a God? We can neither tell him anything he does not know nor urge him to love more than he already does (a candle may just as well command the sun to shine more brightly), nor can we add one particle to his infinite and endless happiness by our praise. We are pretty much the definition of a kind of cosmic fifth wheel. In light of such a God, our prayer — and indeed our very existence — is utterly superfluous. We are, in the words of Robert Farrar Capon, "radically unnecessary."[4] God not only doesn't need us to pray, but he also doesn't need us to do anything. He doesn't need us to exist at all!

Yet Jesus teaches us to pray and makes his actions, in a certain sense, so dependent on ours that his very instruction on prayer is given because we ask him to tell us how to pray. Why this seeming passivity on the part of him who is Pure Act?

The answer is found in the immense gulf between Jesus' reference to God as "my heavenly Father" and his instruction to us to refer to God as "Our Father." Jesus uses the term "my Father" in a way that makes clear that he enjoys by nature a relationship with God that we do not enjoy. God the Father is the Father of Jesus the Son. Jesus shares the Father's divine nature. Jesus is of the same "God stuff" as the Father. We are not. We are creatures, not sons and daughters. We are related to God as a statue is related to its sculptor, not as a child is related to his parent. Moreover, to complicate matters, we are creatures *in rebellion*. Evil has distanced us from God in ways that merely being a creature never could.

Jesus repeatedly emphasizes that distinct relationship when he tells us things like "You are from below, I am from above" (John 8:23) and when he takes for granted the fact that he is without sin and entirely pleasing to the Father while we are sinners, etc. To be sure, his teaching, particularly in the Sermon on the Mount, insists that we must call God "Father." But the whole point of this language is to make clear that this is shocking and revolutionary.

Occasionally, in the Old Testament, one of the prophets will speak of God as the Father of Israel. Now and then, a psalmist will posit a father/son relationship between God and some dignitary such as a Davidic king. But Jesus makes this the absolutely normative relationship between his followers and his Father. In doing so, he tells us that this is permissible only because he has authorized and commanded us to enter such an intimate relationship with our "Abba" (Romans 8:15-16). The corollary is that without that authorization and command, it would be sheer impudence and effrontery on our part. In short, the clear implication of Jesus' teaching is that, apart from him, we would have no right whatsoever to call God "Father."

That comes as a shock to many people in our post-Christian culture who take it as a natural right simply because the Christian tradition has, for so long, called God "Father." Perhaps that shock is not a bad thing since the Christian revelation *should* shock. Christianity tells us that — not because we are "that kind of chap," but because of the Passion, Death, and Resurrection — a radical change has been wrought by the God-man in the relationship between God and man, so that we can, after eons of estrangement, call God "Father." It declares that after the Resurrection, the One who had hitherto referred to "my Father" in starkly exclusive terms now says to Mary Magdalene, "Go to my brethren and say to them, I am ascending to my Father and your Father, to my God and your God" (John 20:17).

When the Second Adam ascends, humanity is planted squarely in the heart of heaven, and God and man are now reconciled. God is no longer merely the Father of Jesus Christ the Son but of all who believe in him. So, as the Church puts it in the Mass, we "dare" to say, "Our Father." In the words of C. S. Lewis, we are given the right and duty to "dress up as Christ."[5]

That's why prayer is not (and we are not) superfluous to God. For he who needs neither us nor our prayers is nonetheless the God who loves us. And in loving us, he not only utters us into being out of nothing but also raises us to become what St. Peter calls "partakers of the divine nature" (2 Peter 1:4). As the Catholic philosopher and teacher Blaise Pascal observes, God instituted prayer in order to lend us the dignity of being causes. What is more, we are not mere "causes" (a cue ball can be *that*) but sons and daughters in his Son, Christ Jesus.

The grace that lends us our borrowed dignity is always *prior*. Every movement of the heart toward God, no matter how feeble and flickering, occurs because God was already at work in the mysterious depths of our being, moving us toward himself. That's why, at the end of the day, it only *appears* that Jesus was passively revealing himself in response to others' comments and requests. In fact, requests like "Lord, teach us to pray" and insights like "You are the Christ, the Son of the living God" occur, as Jesus himself said, due to the power of his heavenly Father at work in our hearts. As he said, we did not choose him, he chose us (John 15:16).

All of the early struggles to understand the revelation of Christ — the seeking, the questioning, the doubting, and the desiring that the apostles went through in their long, slow, stumbling walk after Jesus — were due ultimately, not to "man's search for God," but to the Good Shepherd who seeks the lost sheep. The apostles cried out "Lord, teach us to pray!" because God put the hunger for him into their hearts, inspired them to freely seek him, and then freely answered them. The prayer "Teach us to pray," simply by being a prayer and not a magic formula, assumed dialogue with God.

Yet, not merely one-on-one dialogue. The Our Father is, paradoxically, an incorrigibly *public* prayer (that's why it's the *Our* Father) to an incorrigibly *intimate* God (which is why Jesus tells us, "But when you pray, go into your room and shut the door and pray to your Father who is in secret; and your Father who sees in secret will reward you" (Matthew 6:6).

What are we to make of a God who reveals himself to be secret, yet simultaneously reveals this prayer to the whole human race? Well, we cannot pretend that the Christian faith is some private, esoteric affair between "me 'n' Jesus." "Our" gives that the lie. To call the Father "Our" and not "My" is to say he is the God of the whole Church, not just of me as an individual. Why then the emphasis on secrecy? Because God meets us as persons in the intimacy of the soul. We approach him in secret because that which is personal is also that which is most universal. For the personal things — like falling in love, fear upon the sea, wonder at the stars, joy at the laughter of children — are not esoteric; they are *common*. But because we are weak, we often cannot reveal ourselves as persons to God in public due to fear of what people will think or the distracting desire to impress them. So God calls us to private prayer in order that we may practice being *persons*, so that in our public practice of the faith, we may share that gift of personhood with others.

Make no mistake; ours is a public faith. Jesus had that in view when he established his Church. The notion that the Christian faith should be "private" in the sense that it should be neither seen nor heard in the public square was as unintelligible to Jesus as it was to the Jewish tradition from which he came. To be sure, acts of piety — such as prayer, fasting, and almsgiving — should not be done in order to gain the praise of human beings. But that's not because "faith is a private thing." Rather, our public witness to the faith must not be compromised by even so much as the appearance of a faith that is offered in sacrifice, not to God our Father, but to public opinion. It is precisely because the Church is a visible body of believers and a sacrament to the world of the mercy and love of God that it must not be tainted by the mercenary attempt to leverage our "spirituality" into something calculated to win acclamation for us.

Winning acclamation for "Our Father" is another thing entirely. That is why Jesus offsets the exhortation to do our acts of piety privately with another, less noticed command to make our faith a very public thing indeed:

> "You are the light of the world. A city set on a hill cannot be hid. Nor do men light a lamp and put it under a bushel, but on a stand, and it gives light to all in the house. Let your light so shine before men, that they may see your good works and give glory to your Father who is in heaven." (Matthew 5:14-16)

Precisely the point of this teaching is that glory is good, so long as we give it to God our Father and don't divert it to ourselves. So Catholics are unabashed in public worship. The Mass is not all about us but about the worship of God the Father in and through Jesus the Son.

That's why the Our Father has always had pride of place at Mass. In the Mass, we live out what Jesus instructs us to do in the Our Father — enter into the total and perfect self-offering of his Son. Once again, we "dress up as Christ" and ride his coattails into heaven by being joined with his life, death, and resurrection, first in the sacrament of Baptism and most profoundly in the sacrament of the Eucharist. We give him our little, broken, creaturely life, and he gives us his "spirit of sonship," whereby we cry, "Abba, Father" (Romans 8:15). Because we are now sons and daughters in the Son, we participate in the life of the Blessed Trinity to such a degree that God, in his providence, actually takes our prayers into account as he continues his single ongoing act of creation and redemption. He chooses to make our prayers matter, for we pray as his own children. And because we are children, we can enter into prayer, not in the muck sweat of a half-panicked fear that a capricious deity might let us starve if we don't get some magic formula recited just right, but in the confidence that Jesus himself had in his heavenly Father. It is this confidence that suffuses the Our Father and steers us, not to a prayer of petition (which is often the first form of prayer that we think of) but to the recognition that our Father is in heaven.

Chapter 2

WHO ART IN HEAVEN

Our Father is not, according to Jesus, merely our Father. He is our Father "who art in heaven." What does that mean?

Getting at the answer to that, in our present culture, is harder than you'd think, not least because heaven, says C. S. Lewis, is an acquired taste. Indeed, there are moments, Lewis notes, when he wonders whether we really desire heaven.

I know how he feels. I grew up as a pagan. That's not to say I grew up worshiping Apollo or painting myself with woad and running around naked in the woods (a vision to conjure with). Rather, it is to say that I grew up unbaptized, almost completely unconnected with the Christian tradition, except what I could glean from *A Charlie Brown Christmas* and the occasional glimpses of *The Robe* at Easter. I came away with dim impressions of something about Romans, peace on earth, violent death, and that schmaltzy 1950s-era portrayal of sanctity, with choirs of angels and people suddenly gazing off into the distance with a look of profound awe. I knew that Christmas was Jesus' birthday. I did not know what Easter was about until sometime in my teens. My grasp of Scripture came from one abortive attempt at age thirteen to read Genesis, where I started at chapter 1, plowed on through to Genesis 3, gave it up, ruffled the pages of the Bible till I found the book of Revelation (turns out it's in the back), gave that a stab, and then closed the thing, with my head spinning.

Modern-day Christianity, which was only tenuously connected in my mind with "Bible stories," was a vague amalgam of holier-than-thou hypocrites from preachy '70s sitcoms (St. Frank Burns, pray for us!); chilly Lutheran devotional art on the walls of the local rest home; sundry "born again" fellow students in high school, whose awkward attempts to "witness" to me just made me feel awkward; and various encounters with scary Christians like Jack Chick, assorted TV screamers, and the drawings of Gustave Doré (Noah's flood and Dante in hell: brrrrr!). When I was four years old, I somehow picked up from a Paine Field AFB Vacation Bible School the notion that you shouldn't say Jesus' name. Once, in high school, I darkened the door of a Catholic church when a friend asked me to come to Good Friday services. I had not one clue what was going on.

Bottom line: When I thought of "religion," I didn't even think about it long enough to dismiss it. It just seemed unconnected to me. While I suppose I hoped vaguely for something pleasant to happen in an afterlife — rather than, say, discovering that H. P. Lovecraft was horrifyingly right — I didn't give it much thought one way or the other. "Christian heaven" seemed mostly boring, consisting of white clouds, harps, and the singing of dull "church songs" of the type led by schoolmarms in old Westerns. Mostly I felt (and when left to my natural inclinations, unenlightened by revelation, still feel) a foreboding that at death you simply go out like a light and that nothing happens after your final agonies. My normal natural mood is to veer toward the general suspicion that death, rather than life, is a tale told by an idiot, full of sound and fury, signifying nothing.

Not that I have ever been an atheist. Atheists have always struck me as being a sort of photo negative of "Scary Christians" like Chick. They have a certitude and a diagrammatic worldview I lack. They are way angry, as a rule, arguing in ways that typically say, "There is no God," but which feel like "Hell, yes, there's a God, and I'm hissing mad at him!"

No, it's always been death, not life, that seemed idiotic to me. I can easily believe in a meaningful life, and being a pagan only whetted that inescapable sense of a world bursting at the seams with hidden meaning. As a pagan, I had a reverence for the unseen and unknown. That included God. Growing up, I had the weird impression that everything I could see around me would, if I could just get around *behind* it, reveal an entire unseen world. It was as though all creation was a sort of stage set, and on the other side of it was Reality. I remember listening to a Jethro Tull album in the late '70s and feeling the dim sense that the blasphemies and insults Ian Anderson directed against God were not so much wrong as dangerous. (Don't irritate The Power behind things.)

Of course, being unknown, this unseen Power was also scary and not a God of love as Christians understand him. The Power behind things *might* be something more like a fate than a god: a capricious (and should it turn its gaze on me, *malignant*) Will or Presence that was setting the universe up as a vast practical joke to be sprung on me when I finally let my guard down. Oddly, I didn't consider that a blasphemous thought. I thought it was a cautious (and dreadful) thought, the thought of a helpless victim and not of a rebellious sinner. I hoped that the Power wasn't like that. But something in my Irish makeup tended toward such pessimism and flirtation with despair.

I give you all of this boring autobiography because it is the interior life of millions of people around the world who likewise live in a pagan universe haunted by the unknown God. It is precisely to such minds that the stunning revelation that our Father is in *heaven* is addressed, with the incredible prospect that, so far from living in a horror movie where the hero wakes from the nightmare and finds that his waking reality is worse, faith teaches us that every fairy-tale hope that has ever stirred our hearts might actually be realized and that, quite literally, all our wishes might come true.

This hope, that there might really be, at the end of all things, what J. R. R. Tolkien called "Joy, Joy beyond the walls of the world, poignant as grief,"[6] is what Jesus is getting at when he tells us our Father is a *heavenly* Father. It answers profoundly another element in pagan life that I experienced countless times, forming a sort of leitmotif of my pre-Christian life. It was a thing I kept well under wraps for the simple reason that it was an experience that lies right at the root of who I am, and it formed the underpinning of every good desire, action, and choice I have ever made. It was an experience so intensely personal to me that I did not talk about it, even with myself. I figured I was, well, crazy, and I would no more have brought it up in casual conversation than I would have gone for a stroll buck naked in a shopping mall. Indeed, I might still be a pagan had I not made the acquaintance of a great writer named C. S. Lewis, who had plucked up the courage to say: You are not alone. I also have experienced, not so much the presence as the absence of that "unnameable something, desire for which pierces us like a rapier at the smell of a bonfire, the sound of wild ducks flying overhead, the title of *The Well at the World's End*, the opening lines of *Kubla Kahn*, the morning cobwebs in late summer, or the noise of falling waves."[7]

Lewis called it by various names: Desire, Joy, *sehnsucht*, the appetite for heaven. He wrote about it in words that still bring tears to my eyes, making clear that the seeming lack of desire for heaven was mere illusion:

> There have been times when I think we do not desire heaven; but more often I find myself wondering whether, in our heart of hearts, we ever desired anything else. You may have noticed that the books you really love are bound together by a secret thread. You know very well what is the common quality that makes you love them, though you cannot put it into words: but most of your friends do not see it at all, and often wonder why, liking this, you should also like that. . . . Are not all lifelong friendships born at the moment when at last you meet another human being who has some inkling (but faint and uncertain even in the best) of that something which you were born desiring, and which, beneath the flux of other desires and in all the momentary silences between the louder passions, night and day, year by year, from childhood to old age, you are looking for, watching for, listening for? You

have never *had* it. . . . But if it should really become manifest
. . . you would know it. Beyond all possibility of doubt you
would say, "Here at last is the thing I was made for." We cannot tell each other about it. It is the secret signature of each
soul, the incommunicable and unappeasable want, the thing
we desired before we met our wives or made our friends or
chose our work, and which we shall still desire on our death-
beds, when the mind no longer knows wife or friend or work.
While we are, this is. If we lose this, we lose all.[8]

Lewis made an instant friend of me because he was describ-
ing perfectly my deepest interior experience growing up. Only he
didn't just describe it; he made sense of it:

Creatures are not born with desires unless satisfaction for
those desires exists. A baby feels hunger; well, there is such a
thing as food. A duckling wants to swim; well, there is such
a thing as water. Men feel sexual desire; well, there is such a
thing as sex. *If I find in myself a desire which no experience in
this world can satisfy, the most probable explanation is that I
was made for another world.* If none of my earthly pleasures
satisfy it, that does not prove that the universe is a fraud.
Probably earthly pleasures were never meant to satisfy it, but
only to arouse it, to suggest the real thing.[9]

This, at long last, made sense both of the longing and of the
frustration of this passing world. There really is Something behind
it all. But the Something is not a capricious power or a malicious
joker. It is not an It at all, but a He — the source of all the beauty
and the ultimate fulfillment of all desire. Indeed, precisely the reason creation was "subjected to futility" (Romans 8:20) is so that
we, who are so prone to doing so, would not batten on it and seek
to satisfy ourselves with it. He has "put eternity into man's mind"
(Ecclesiastes 3:11) and arranged all things so that "our hearts are
restless till they find rest in Thee," as Augustine said.[10]

Of course, mere desire is not a proof of sanctity. It is merely a proof of humanity. My point is not to illustrate Lewis' (and still less my) cause for canonization. Rather, it is to make clear that, in fact, the hunger for heaven is indeed a burning fire in our hearts and that Jesus really is addressing something right at the core of our being when he tells us that our Father is in heaven. It's not sugary religious talk but a statement of fact about who God really is — everlasting ecstasy, the fulfillment of our deepest longings, the hope toward which all our little hopes flow as tiny rivulets join larger streams till they pour out as a mighty river into the endless sea of his glory. When Jesus calls us to address our Father in this way, he models for us (and assists us in emulating him) the setting of our minds, right from the start, on heavenly realities — which are the real story — and taking our distracted hearts and minds off earthly frippery.

In doing so, he prepares us to do the main thing that prayer is about, which is not "asking for stuff" (though that's part of it), but is instead speaking forth the praise of his glory in the words "hallowed be thy name."

Chapter 3

HALLOWED BE THY NAME

The refugees returning to the Promised Land after seventy years of captivity in Babylon had a problem. He was a spoilsport named Haggai, and he was chewing them out for rebuilding their houses.

Well, that's not exactly the case. His complaint wasn't so much that the Israelites were rebuilding their homes as that they were doing this without so much as a thought to the God who had brought them back from captivity, in direct fulfillment of the promises he had made to them. Haggai's point was not "God is a killjoy" but rather "God demands that we put him first in our lives — not treat him as an afterthought once things begin to turn around for us." So he cried, "Is it a time for you yourselves to dwell in your paneled houses, while this house lies in ruins?" (Haggai 1:4).

"This house" refers to the Temple in Jerusalem, and the verse sums up the message of the prophet to the gloomy, dispirited Jews who had returned from the Babylonian Exile to find their city a pile of rubble, their temple a heap of stones, and their future a bleak blank. Being fallen humans, they set about taking care of *numero uno*, as their fathers had done before them. Haggai's task was to remind them that God's temple, not their dining-room set, was *numero uno* and that they should remember, as an earlier prophet had said: "If you are unfaithful, I will scatter you among the peoples; but if you return to me and keep my commandments and do them, though your dispersed be under the farthest skies, I will gather them thence and bring them to the place which I have chosen, to make my name dwell there" (Nehemiah 1:8-9).

In short, neither the Jewish people's exile nor their return was simply an accident but was instead the fulfillment of the covenant promises made by God Almighty to the children of Israel at Mount Sinai. It was God and his covenant that were the real center of the story, not the people's real-estate development projects. If they wanted to actually live happily (as distinct from simply continuing with a sort of ancient rat-race existence), they needed to correct their vision so as to see God and put him first in their lives. In the words of the Messiah, who would eventually come and build the *real* temple of which the Jerusalem temple was just a dim shadow, they had to learn to "seek first his kingdom and his righteousness, and all these things shall be yours as well" (Matthew 6:33).

We are in the same boat as Haggai's exiles. That's why, when our culture thinks of prayer, it tends to think first of "asking for stuff." If we pop in the prayer coin and get the car, job, spouse, or sundry goody, then prayer "worked." Conversely, if we don't get all the stuff we want, many people conclude that prayer "doesn't work." Undergirding this notion of prayer is the conception of God as a cosmic vending machine rather than as a Trinity of Persons with whom we have a relationship.

Now, as we shall see in future chapters, there is most certainly a place for petitionary prayer in the Christian tradition. Throughout both Scripture and Church history, the saints have not merely asked for stuff but for quite outrageous stuff, up to and including multiplication of loaves and fishes and life for dead people sans pulse and brainwave. Scripture has not a word to say against people asking God for all sorts of stuff.

But there is no room, none whatever, for praying as though God is a machine. Instead, as Jesus instructs us in the Our Father, the very first order of business is to usher us into the covenant relationship God has desired with us ever since he made Adam and Eve in his image and likeness. Even in the midst of our most urgent need, not to mention in the midst of our day-to-day "daily bread" needs, Jesus throws up a roadblock to our urge to rush on to the "asking for stuff" part of prayer. Instead, he calls us to remember the One to whom we are speaking and to enter into the highest form of language the human person can participate in: the language of praise and thanksgiving to God.

Therefore, long before we ever get to "Give us this day our daily bread" or "Deliver us from evil," we are urged to take a good look at God for who he is. When we do that, we find Our Father's "Name" is hallowed. What does that mean?

Jewish piety has always seen a colossal significance in names, and nowhere more so than in the Name of God himself. Among the Ten Commandments (and well before you get to the natural-law stuff about killing, adultery and theft) you find the command, "You shall not take the name of the LORD your God in vain; for the LORD will not hold him guiltless who takes his name in vain" (Exodus 20:7).

In Scripture, the name (and supremely God's Name) is a deeply sacred thing. It is not just a label slapped on a thing so that we can call it something besides a thingamajig. For the biblical authors, a name — and especially a person's name — somehow expressed his essence. To know someone's name was to know *him*. To name, or rename, someone was to effect and reflect a fundamental change in who he was. To use the Name of God, therefore, was a solemn thing and not to be taken lightly. To bless the Name of God was to be taken up into the divine work of the angels. To bear the Name of God was to become, in some sense, a member of the family of God. To hallow God's Name as Jesus commands us to do was (and remains) the highest form of prayer that a human being can offer with his lips. It is to say, in mere sound, what Jesus would say with his very body and blood in his passion, crucifixion, and death.

That's why this petition always comes first. Jesus wants us to love his Father as he does and to ingrain into our very bones the truth that the Father is more important than anything else. It is his Kingdom, not our wish list, that matters. It is his will that must be done, not ours. In learning the Lord's Prayer, we learn the right order of things and are taught a bit about how not to be fools who put second things first and first things last. In so doing, we start our prayer, not by building our own house, but by becoming living stones and making the place that he has chosen to make his Name dwell, the temple which is the Body of Christ.

Chapter 4

THY KINGDOM COME

A modernist scholar once complained that Jesus came to proclaim the Kingdom of God, but instead all we got was this lousy Church. He's not the only person to have felt a bit disappointed nor the only one to form the conviction that the Church is a tragic letdown, a mistake, and not something Jesus ever intended. One seldom looks around one's local parish and is filled with the awestruck feeling, "Behold! The Kingdom!" It's one of the things Uncle Screwtape rather enjoys banging away at, as he tells his nephew Wormwood:

> One of our great allies at present is the Church itself. Do not misunderstand me. I do not mean the Church as we see her spread out through all time and space and rooted in eternity, terrible as an army with banners. That, I confess, is a spectacle which makes our boldest tempters uneasy. But fortunately it is quite invisible to these humans. All your patient sees is the half-finished, sham Gothic erection on the new building estate. When he goes inside, he sees the local grocer with rather an oily expression on his face bustling up to offer him one shiny little book containing a liturgy which neither of them understands, and one shabby little book containing corrupt texts of a number of religious lyrics, mostly bad, and in very small print. When he gets to his pew and looks round him he sees just that selection of his neighbours whom he has hitherto avoided. You want to lean pretty heavily on those neighbours. Make his mind flit to and fro between an expression like "the body of Christ" and the actual faces in the next pew. It matters very little, of course, what kind of people that next pew really contains. You may know one of

them to be a great warrior on the Enemy's side. No matter. Your patient, thanks to Our Father Below, is a fool.[11]

This odd tendency to mistake the merely pictorial for the spiritual is all over the place, I fear, in our current approach to the faith. We imagine we are being spiritual, but really we have this vague notion that the "Kingdom of God" should somehow be a sort of egalitarian co-op of shining saints and folks affirming one another in their okayness, all in union with a Jesus who is not so much "Lord" as "Wise and Strong Affirmer of our Basic Goodness." Certainly, much of the American Catholic Church is afflicted with this vision, leading to a celebration of the liturgy that author Amy Welborn has puckishly described as the Rite of the Church of Aren't We Fabulous.

You've probably had to endure, at some point, a "sacred meal" where we gather around the Table to celebrate our Us-ness because it's all about Us. We come to share our story, not humble ourselves before the Gospel. We come to break the bread, not the body, blood, soul and divinity of Jesus Christ fully present in the Most Holy Sacrifice of the altar. We come to know our rising from the dead, without the nasty business of taking up crosses. Some of our trendier talking heads speak of the "reign of God" and assure us that the crucifixion of Jesus was a tragic accident, not part of the plan of God at all. We are taught by some to see the liturgy as a time when we come to discover yet again that we are superior to all previous generations as, for instance, in a homily I once endured in which the priest informed us that even Jesus had to "learn to overcome his racism." Along with this celebration of our superior Us-ness, we banish all those dark pre-Vatican II notions of sin, humility, and sacrifice, except for the sake of self-empowerment and toned abs, and assert our "dignity," a word that sounds an awful lot like "pride" in the mouths of suburban Americans.

In short, we in the American Church start by talking about the "Kingdom" but somehow quickly end by talking about the People's

Democratic Republic of Heaven, free of odious and (this must be said with a sneer) "medieval" notions of hierarchy, authority, and so forth.

Given that Jesus' conception of the Kingdom seems (in stark contrast) to have something to do with founding rather than fleeing from the Church, my suggestion for repairing the increasingly stark disconnect between AmChurch Cath Lite and the actual Church (and Kingdom) is to return to the language of Jesus and, in particular, to what words like "kingdom" actually mean in the minds of Jesus and his apostles. When we do that, we discover that before Jesus and his apostles look forward to the coming of the Kingdom, they have their minds rooted in the past and, in particular, focused on one king. It is King David and his kingly line that lie at the root of the entire Jewish conception of the Messiah.

For the Messiah is no one and nothing other than the Son of David. The entire Jewish conception of the Messiah rests on the conviction that God will make good on a promise given to David after he was made king of the people of Israel by popular acclaim and began to reign in Jerusalem. The language of that popular acclamation was, as we shall see, significant. But even more significant is the nature of the covenant God makes with King David after he seeks counsel from the prophet Nathan on whether he should build a "house" (i.e., temple) for the Lord. Nathan replies to him with this astonishing prophecy:

> "Go and tell my servant David, 'Thus says the Lord: Would you build me a house to dwell in? I have not dwelt in a house since the day I brought up the people of Israel from Egypt to this day, but I have been moving about in a tent for my dwelling. In all places where I have moved with all the people of Israel, did I speak a word with any of the judges of Israel, whom I commanded to shepherd my people Israel, saying, "Why have you not built me a house of cedar?" ' Now therefore thus you shall say to my servant David, 'Thus says the

LORD of hosts, I took you from the pasture, from following the sheep, that you should be prince over my people Israel; and I have been with you wherever you went, and have cut off all your enemies from before you; and I will make for you a great name, like the name of the great ones of the earth. And I will appoint a place for my people Israel, and will plant them, that they may dwell in their own place, and be disturbed no more; and violent men shall afflict them no more, as formerly, from the time that I appointed judges over my people Israel; and I will give you rest from all your enemies. Moreover the LORD declares to you that the LORD will make you a house. When your days are fulfilled and you lie down with your fathers, I will raise up your offspring after you, who shall come forth from your body, and I will establish his kingdom. He shall build a house for my name, and I will establish the throne of his kingdom for ever. I will be his father, and he shall be my son. When he commits iniquity, I will chasten him with the rod of men, with the stripes of the sons of men; but I will not take my steadfast love from him, as I took it from Saul, whom I put away from before you. And your house and your kingdom shall be made sure for ever before me; your throne shall be established for ever.' " (2 Samuel 7:5-16)

The punning triple promise that (1) God will build David a "house" (i.e., a dynasty), (2) that David's son "shall build a house for my name," and (3) "I will establish the throne of his kingdom for ever" is the source of the entire Messianic concept. The worldly failure of the House of David and its destruction by the Babylonian Conquest serves, paradoxically, only to sharpen the expectation that the promise to David cannot fail. Even though, politically, the Davidic line loses the political throne, and as the First Temple is destroyed, Judah's hope in the promise to David only grows.

This hope would seem to be hugely delusional by the first century A.D. After all, the Jews are, by the time of Christ, ruled not by a Jewish king but by an Idumaean named Herod and then (worse still) by a Roman named Pontius Pilate. In a similar vein of apparently mocking failure by the muse of history, Ezekiel had prophesied a rebuilt temple as a sign of a restored covenant, yet Herod's temple was no more the work of a Son of David than the Nashville, Tennessee, Parthenon was the work of ancient Greeks. None of the prophetic promises seemed to be panning out at all. Prophecy appeared to be a joke.

All this led popular Judaism to get some things right and some things disastrously wrong. In the "getting it right" department is pre-Christian Judaism's valiant will to retain the Messianic idea at all. There's a reason you haven't met any Amorites, Perizzites, Sumerians, or Hittites. They're gone. They had no vision, and they perished. But the Jews, by divine Providence and an iron will, stuck to their hope in the words of the prophets and believed that the Messiah would come. For this, we are forever in their debt.

The problem is that when the Messiah came, the Kingdom he proclaimed was not what they expected. No conquering king to beat up the Gentiles and kick them out of the Holy Land. Not much in the way of hamstrung horses or collections of large numbers of foreskins from dead opponents as David had done (1 Samuel 18:25-27). The brave band of followers turned out to be fishermen, tax collectors, and whores, not David's mighty men. Quite un-Davidic — or so it seemed.

To be sure, the Messiah claimed, both explicitly and implicitly, to be the king of Israel. He even rode into Jerusalem on a donkey (Matthew 21:1-10) as Solomon had done a thousand years earlier (1 Kings 1:43-44), when he laid claim to the Davidic throne (a gesture not lost on any of his countrymen), which is why, hopes high, they shouted "Hosanna!" They thought the Revolution and the New Davidic Kingdom would be any minute now. They were absolutely right — and horribly wrong.

Just how right and wrong was soon apparent. The Son of David started doing weird stuff: identifying himself with a mysterious "bridegroom" (Matthew 25:1-13) as well as with some king who would come at the end of time to judge us on our treatment of "the least of these" (Matthew 25:31-46). He asked unsettling questions about Psalm 110 (universally regarded by his contemporaries as both Davidic in origin and Messianic in nature) and pointed out that David called the Son of David "Lord" (Matthew 22:41-45). He ticked off the power elites who had gotten pretty cozy with the army of the occupation (Matthew 23) and who didn't want to rock the boat with miracle stories about his raising the dead (John 11:45-53). And when it came to the Temple? Talk about disrespect for religious decorum! Would David have ever cleared out the moneychangers and treated such a venerable national institution with such rabble-rousing fury (Matthew 21:12)?

Clearly, said the top people, the man was a pretender to the throne, and clearly he had said and done enough to hang himself. His claims to kingship were so well known by the time he was brought to trial that both Pilate and the Sanhedrin could make them the basis for the prosecution. Yes, mixed in with the Son of David stuff was other weird business about destroying the Temple and raising it in three days (John 2:19). (They weren't sure what that meant, but they tossed it into the indictment and brought forward a few massaged witnesses ready to spin his words, in the hope that some sort of terrorism charge would stick (Mark 14:57-59). And he did exude a disquieting uncanniness when he warned of returning on clouds of glory and took the Name "I AM" to himself (Mark 14:61-62) (which was the real crime as far as the Sanhedrin was concerned). But with practiced calm, his accusers stuck with the claim of kingship, since that's what Rome would care about.

Of course, that eerie "I AM" claim almost torpedoed the whole project when the superstitious Pilate, spooked by his wife's dream (Matthew 27:19), remembered old myths of gods who came to earth in disguise and vented their wrath on the puny mortals who mistreated them. He asked, "Where are you from?" and then blustered, "Do you not know that I have power to release you, and power to crucify you?" (John 19:9-10). But the man with the crown of thorns seemed in no danger of erupting in Olympian fury and eventually, with a bit of pressure from the Sanhedrin warning that if Pilate freed this man claiming to be Christ, *a king*, he was "not Caesar's friend" (John 19:12), Pilate plucked up the courage to have his horsewhipped prisoner traded off for some two-bit hood named Barabbas and disposed of two other pieces of trash awaiting execution in the Tower of Antonia.

The rest we know, except that we don't know it, because we don't think of what happened, as the apostles and Jesus did. Oh sure, we acknowledge the story of the Passion as truth. But sooner or later the story ends, our eyes refocus, and we look around at our adult Sunday school class, there in the air-conditioned room, with the fluorescent lights and the little table with coffee and Oreos on it, and we think: "So it was all leading up to *this* and the Church social with the fruit salad we had last night?" In short, we think of the Church as a sort of afterthought to the whole drama of the crucifixion, resurrection, and ascension of Jesus. A mere "human institution" cooked up by "mere men," who basically needed something to kill the time while they waited around for Jesus to come back.

But Jesus thinks in a different way. He thinks of the Church as the whole point of the Crucifixion, Resurrection, and Ascension. The Church is, in fullness, what the kingdom of David was in foreshadow. The promise of the Law and the prophets — including the prophet called David — has been fulfilled, as Jesus himself told the disciples on the Emmaus road.

So, for instance, we discover that the Kingdom is nuptial, just as the Davidic kingdom was. The Davidic kingdom is inaugurated with language that comes from the most primal union in the history of the human race: "Then all the tribes of Israel came to David at Hebron, and said, 'Behold, we are your *bone and flesh*'" (2 Samuel 5:1, emphasis added). If that "bone and flesh" imagery sounds like a conscious reference to the language of Genesis — "This at last is bone of my bones and flesh of my flesh" (Genesis

2:23) — that's because it is. This idea of the Davidic king as a sort of Adam to Israel's Eve is recapitulated by the Son of David when he inaugurates his public ministry at a wedding (John 2:1-11). The sign he gives at that feast is Eucharistic: changing water into wine in anticipation of the great Eucharistic feast, which is itself nuptial in that it foreshadows the "marriage supper of the Lamb" (Revelation 19:9) at the consummation of all things.

And in case we still don't connect the dots, the forerunner of Jesus, John the Baptist, spells it out for us on the next page when he says that Jesus is the Bridegroom in the great Messianic wedding (John 3:29-30). That wedding is with none other than the Church, who is the true Bride of Christ. The marriage is consummated when the side of the Second Adam, hanging beneath a titulus declaring him to be "Jesus of Nazareth, the King of the Jews," is pierced on the cross, and from his side come blood and water (John 19:19, 34). John the Evangelist doesn't tell us this because he thought we'd be interested in the medical details of pericardial rupture. He tells us this because this is the moment at which the sacrament of Baptism is inaugurated, and the Church, the bride of the Second Adam, is, like the bride of the first Adam, made from his side: born again in "the Spirit, the water, and the blood" (1 John 5:6-8).

In the same way, Jesus fulfills the Davidic promise of a king as the warrior who defends Israel. However, he does so, not by laying down his life in battle for mere plots of land and political power, but for the most contested real estate in the universe: the human heart. In Isaiah 52:13-53:12, we find the "servant of the Lord" (another title for the Messiah, or Son of David) offering his life in perfection, not merely for the political triumph of his people, but for their complete redemption from sin and death.

> Surely he has borne our griefs and carried our sorrows; yet we esteemed him stricken, smitten by God, and afflicted. But he was wounded for our transgressions, he was bruised for our iniquities; upon him was the chastisement that made us

whole, and with his stripes we are healed. All we like sheep have gone astray; we have turned every one to his own way; and the Lord has laid on him the iniquity of us all. (Isaiah 53:4-6)

In Psalm 110, we likewise find Jesus completely fulfilling the promise made to the Son of David that he would be a priest forever according to the line of Melchizedek, sharing in a priesthood more ancient and profound than that of the Levitical priesthood — a priesthood that is, again, ordered toward the Eucharist and the eternal outpouring of his life for all the people.

In short, the understanding of the Kingdom looks back to the Davidic kingdom before it looks forward to the final coming of the King at the end of time. That's why the Church is not a distraction or declension from the Kingdom but rather the concrete expression of the Eucharistic Davidic Kingdom on earth — now, today. It is not, of course, the final fulfillment of that Kingdom promise. That will not happen until the Last Day, when the King returns and sin, hell, and death are finally and completely defeated. But neither is it something other than or opposite from the Davidic kingdom Jesus preached whenever he spoke of the Kingdom of God. It is the now-and-not-yet Kingdom. And because it is, it is present in the fully restored Davidic temple, made not by hands but from living stones built together into a spiritual house — the house of the Son of King David (1 Peter 2:1-10). So the Kingdom and the Church are inseparably fused in the minds of Jesus and the apostles: for where the Church is, there is the Eucharistic King; and where the King is, there is the Kingdom already present and yet still to come.

That is why, as we shall see, we pray for the Kingdom to come and for God's will to be done on earth, as it is in heaven.

Chapter 5

THY WILL BE DONE

Years ago, a friend's brother was at Reed College in Oregon. It's one of those schools where the students seem to major in protesting more than in actual studying. After several months of watching silly demonstrations about every conceivable PC cause, the guy decided to create one of his own, just to see how many earnest young suckers he could get involved. So he painted a number of signs, cooked up some chants and jingles, and then started recruiting students for his rally. He gathered quite a gaggle of activists from the ranks of the student body, who dutifully went out at his bidding and began the protest. His theme: "NO BAD THINGS! DOWN WITH BAD THINGS!"

I think of this when I contemplate the Lord's Prayer because it can sometimes seem like Jesus proposes something like an angelic inversion of the rather obvious point being made in that silly and satirical rally when he commands us to pray "Thy will be done" to the Father. It is not unreasonable to ask, with respect, "What else *should* we pray for than that God's will be done? Who *isn't* in favor of good things and opposed to bad things?"

I think the answer comes to us very quickly the moment we attempt to get specific. Granted, we want to do God's will, just as we want to get rid of "bad things." But what exactly and concretely does that *mean* here and now?

If we are like most people, we sort of go into vapor lock at this point. Indeed, it's easier to list various bad things we'd like to get rid of than to state positively what we think "God's will" is. I suspect that most of us start with ourselves and our circumstances when trying to discern such matters: What is the will of God for my life? Does God want me to stay in my current job or try for that new one? Get the Ford or the Toyota? Pray more or work harder? Vote for Smith or Jones? Have faith for a miraculous healing for Mother's cancer or ask for the grace to accept the suffering that is coming?

All day long we muddle along trying to figure out God's will and feeling slightly silly about it because, after all, who really expects God to reveal his will about whether you should get the red or the blue shirt? If we actually meet people who *are* really confident that they are tuned in to the divine frequency and are doing God's will throughout the day ("God showed me that I should pick the creamed corn, not the whole kernel, at Top Foods"), we generally have the sense that we are in the presence of somebody who needs to cut back on the caffeine. So while we approve of "doing God's will" as a general principle, we're not at all sure what that actually means on a day-to-day basis.

This is where revelation and the guidance of the Church really come in handy. The Church, in fact, insists that we *can* know and definitely state certain truths about the will of God. For instance, Our Father "desires all men to be saved and to come to the knowledge of the truth" (1 Timothy 2:3-4). He "is forbearing toward you, not wishing that any should perish" (2 Peter 3:9; cf. Matthew 18:14). His commandment is "that you love one another; even as I have loved you, that you also love one another" (John 13:34; cf. 1 John 3, 4; Luke 10:25-37). This commandment summarizes all the others and expresses his entire will. As the *Catechism of the Catholic Church* puts it:

> "He has made known to us the mystery of his will, according to his good pleasure that he set forth in Christ . . . to gather up all things in him, things in heaven and things on earth. In Christ we have also obtained an inheritance, having been destined according to the purpose of him who accomplishes all things according to his counsel and will" (Ephesians 1:9-11). We ask insistently for this loving plan to be fully realized on earth as it is already in heaven. (CCC 2823)

This is where we begin: with the definite fact that God wills to save us, that he wills us to love one another as he has loved us, and that (mysteriously) his will, in Christ, is to "unite all things in him, things in heaven and things on earth" (Ephesians 1:9-11). It is here that we start. For it is Christ, not our particular perception of our particular circumstances, that really is the central story. We orbit him, not he us.

The striking thing to notice about "Thy will be done" is that it is a *prayer* — a volitional act and even a participatory act. In some religions, even some forms of Christianity, the will of God tends to be seen as something that cancels out human freedom in a sort of zero-sum game, where the more space God takes up, the less space there is for us. Such a conception of the will of God smacks of the inexorable, and our place before it is to submit as a slave to the overwhelming power of a master. In some religious systems, the will of God is literally all there is. Everything that occurs happens because God positively willed it, and our only task is to cringe and call it good, no matter how evil it is. In such systems, the will of God arbitrarily pulls your name out of the inscrutable divine lottery, and if you are chosen, then that's that. The irresistible grace overwhelms you, and you can't help but be saved. If not, too bad for you. God created you because he wills to damn you. The good news is reduced to the proclamation that "God *might* love you and *may* have sent his Son to die for your sins — if you are lucky enough to be among the elect." Your will in the matter is irrelevant.

In contrast to this is the Catholic Gospel, which insists that "where the Spirit of the Lord is, there is freedom" (2 Corinthians 3:17). In other words, precisely *because* the Lord is present, we have real freedom to receive or reject him, to do his will or not. That's why we pray — because we need his help to do what he commands. Indeed, we need his help even to desire to pray to do as he commands. But as we pray, we become participants, real divinized participants, in the life of the Blessed Trinity at work in the world

— and all while remaining the fully human creatures and persons we are. It is the miracle of actually having our cake and eating it too.

This is the origin of one of the more obscure Christological controversies in the history of the Church: the question of whether Jesus has one will or two. It would seem that this arcane matter could only be of interest to tightly wound medieval theologians, but really it has everything to do with us ordinary schlubs. If Jesus has no human will of his own, then he's not our help or guide when he chooses to obey the Father, because he is not fully human. But in fact, being fully human and not just a God who is playacting, Jesus fully enters into the anguish that we have to go through when we make the hard but right choice. When he sweats blood and gasps out the resolution, "Not my will, but yours be done," in Gethsemane, we really can know that he's been there and, moreover, that he is still there for us when we need to face the bitter cross. He really is fully human and fully God; that's why he can save us.

"Thy will be done" is, first and foremost then, a prayer of obedience. But it is the obedience of a child to a Father, not of a craven slave to Tash the Inexorable.[12] Jesus makes a choice in Gethsemane — "Father, if thou art willing, remove this cup from me; nevertheless not my will, but thine, be done" (Luke 22:42) — and we are called to make the same choice in little, tiny ways each day, until it all is consummated in the final offering of our life to the Father through Christ. Shockingly, Scripture tells us that Jesus "learned obedience through what he suffered" (Hebrews 5:8), a statement that makes no sense unless we again grant the full humanity of Christ. When we do, it gives us great hope because it means that God the Son really has borne the fullness of the heartache we bear as we struggle to say yes to the hard work of death to self inherent in "Thy will be done."

That said, Jesus' perfect human will means more than simply "he's been there." It means that he can help us get to where he is. For as universal human experience makes clear, "uniting our will to God's" sounds great, but in the words of the *Catechism*, we are "radically incapable of this" (CCC 2825). Grace is always prior for us, because without it, we (and the entire created order) could not so much as exist, much less will what God wills. For in addition to the fact that we are creatures, we are also *fallen* creatures: creatures who have rebelled against our Creator, who don't want to know him, who are terrified of knowing him, and who, when we get the chance, nail him to a cross when he enters into our world. We are one messed-up species. Our predicament is just this: the more we need to repent, the less able we are to do it. And boy, do we need to repent, as any glance at the headlines — or the mirror — will make clear.

This is why God became man. Not merely to provide an example but to give us power to do what we cannot do on our own. As Paul puts it:

> God has done what the law, weakened by the flesh, could not do: sending his own Son in the likeness of sinful flesh and for sin, he condemned sin in the flesh, in order that the just requirement of the law might be fulfilled in us, who walk not according to the flesh but according to the Spirit. For those who live according to the flesh set their minds on the things of the flesh, but those who live according to the Spirit set their minds on the things of the Spirit. To set the mind on the flesh is death, but to set the mind on the Spirit is life and peace. For the mind that is set on the flesh is hostile to God; it does not submit to God's law, indeed it cannot; and those who are in the flesh cannot please God.
>
> But you are not in the flesh, you are in the Spirit, if in fact the Spirit of God dwells in you. Any one who does not have the Spirit of Christ does not belong to him. But if Christ is in you, although your bodies are dead because of sin, your spirits are alive because of righteousness. If the Spirit of him who raised Jesus from the dead dwells in you,

he who raised Christ Jesus from the dead will give life to your mortal bodies also through his Spirit which dwells in you. (Romans 8:3-11)

We are enabled to do God's will because God has assumed human nature; put to death the sin that infected it, by a perfect act of surrender to God's will; raised it from the dead; and glorified it. Man is already in heaven in the person of Jesus Christ, and now the God-man can give us the power to recapitulate what he has done through the Holy Spirit. By our lonesome selves, that would be impossible. But as we rely on the grace the Holy Spirit gives through the sacraments, and as we trust him to guide us on a daily basis by our efforts to obey the law of love, God can be depended upon to help us do what he desires: his will, which is love.

None of this is to say that we must only settle for generalities about God's will and cannot know specifics. The Christian tradition is chockablock with the reality of specific guidance given by the Holy Spirit to his people. I even mean guidance of the "Yes, go in that doorway/No, get the creamed corn" variety when it is really necessary to fulfilling the law of love. The world resounds with the testimony of Christians who, setting out to do the law of love, have received very clear and specific indications from God about what the next practical step should be.

How do they do this? Most of the time, the guidance comes in the form of the practice of the virtues (especially prudence), the use of common sense, and through reliance on the tutelage of the Church in the midst of specific circumstances. As C. S. Lewis points out, God loves platitudes and common sense. Of a proposed course of action, he generally urges us to ask very simple questions, such as "Is it righteous?" "Is it prudent?" "Is it possible?" and not "Is this how popular opinion is trending on Twitter?"

But of course, as Scripture points out, there exist other wills in the universe besides those of God and ours — demonic, as well as human wills bent on deception. And deception can be rather easy in our case since we are fallen and our own wills are divided. That is why prayer is described as a "battle" in the *Catechism* and why Jesus so often insists that we apply ourselves to the struggle of prayer. Prayer is one of the principal means by which God purifies us and brings us through to the reality of a single will where we know the freedom and joy of St. Francis, who says with simplicity: "I want what God wants. That is why I am merry!"

Such reliance on common sense and ordinary human virtue is not meant to deny the reality of the supernatural in prayer. In addition to the common human ways in which God guides us in prayer via prudence, justice, temperance, fortitude, and so forth, he sometimes sees fit to reveal his will via supernatural bells and whistles:

> And they went through the region of Phrygia and Galatia, having been forbidden by the Holy Spirit to speak the word in Asia. And when they had come opposite Mysia, they attempted to go into Bithynia, but the Spirit of Jesus did not allow them; so, passing by Mysia, they went down to Troas. And a vision appeared to Paul in the night: a man of Macedonia was standing beseeching him and saying, "Come over to Macedonia and help us." And when he had seen the vision, immediately we sought to go on into Macedonia, concluding that God had called us to preach the gospel to them. (Acts 16:6-10)

We can ask for such guidance in our day-to-day affairs, but we ought not to demand that God perform special effects as a general rule, lest we neglect the weightier matters of the law and become like the Pharisees who sought signs, not because they lacked them, but because they didn't like where the signs Jesus had already given were pointing. In short, as we seek to know God's will, we should be cautious of the human tendency to seek signs, not in order to find things out, but in order to keep from finding things out.

The great model for us in all this discernment of God's will is the Blessed Virgin, who obeys God's will perfectly by the grace of her Son. In doing so, she stands in a peculiarly helpful place for us because, by divine design, she does something that even Jesus, her Son, cannot do: she shows us what a disciple of Jesus looks like. Mary's yes is the yes, not of the Incarnate Son, but of a disciple who doesn't know what is going to happen next; who doesn't quite understand what is going on when Jesus disappears at the age of twelve, yet who trusts anyway (Luke 2:41-51); who is worried about Jesus' safety when the rumors start flying that he is crazy, and yet trusts (Mark 3:21-35); who has to stand there and watch when her whole world is shattered by the Crucifixion, but does not despair (John 19:25). Hers is the act of saying, "Thy will be done," in that one-foot-in-front-of-the-other way that marks our dark and mysterious path through this world, where we are not shown the whole road but only have light for the next step. Her "Let it be to me according to your word" (Luke 1:38) sums up the whole way of obedience to the will of God.

Mary wills God's will alone. She lives out Kierkegaard's great observation that "Purity of heart is to will one thing"[13] and Dante's great truth, "In his will, our peace."[14] In doing so, she becomes a sort of miniature figurine of the Church, displaying the perfect freedom that comes from perfect obedience to God. For that, of course, is the point of Christian obedience to the will of God: freedom, not enslavement. As Paul says, "For freedom Christ has set us free" (Galatians 5:1). Our freedom is an end, not a means, because we are ends, not means. God did not create and redeem us for some other goal to which we are merely stepping-stones. He has no ulterior motives for our salvation. He does not, as our culture does, treat us like utilitarian tools for some other purpose. Rather, as the Church teaches, man is "the only creature on earth that God has willed for its own sake" (CCC 356). Because of this, obedience to the will of God can be and indeed must be seen as the way toward the full flourishing of the human person according to the law of love. That is why St. Augustine could so cheerily summarize Christian surrender to the will of God this way: "Once for all then, a short precept is given you: Love, and do what you will."[15]

Chapter 6

ON EARTH AS IT IS IN HEAVEN

Our Lord teaches us to pray that God's will be done "on earth, as it is in heaven." But I sometimes fancy that we have seldom given much thought to what that means.

I think that, in part, it's because we don't quite know what to make of heaven, much less how God's will is done there, or how to use that as a template for doing God's will here. The popular notion of heaven is of a sort of pictorial mélange of puffy clouds, pink cherubim, and gauzy TV images of a paradise park or perpetual comfy chair by the hearth on Christmas Eve. Occasionally, in our postmodern culture, our more trendy sorts will depict a God- and angel-free "heaven" of "higher consciousness," in which we achieve something called "enlightenment" and move beyond such petty concerns as love and the troubles of mortal flesh. This usually involves the screen fading to a white blank to signify that the hero has ascended to some realm beyond good and evil, etc. The bottom line is that whether you believe in God or merely in enlightenment, heaven is the place where, as the saying goes, "all our troubles are over."

The problem is, the New Testament doesn't seem to share this simple picture of heaven. Indeed, the puzzle of Scripture is pinning down just what the word "heaven" means. Of course, part of the puzzle is that heaven is something that, in biblical Greek as in modern English, refers to both spiritual and physical reality. Partly, "heaven" or "the heavens" refers to the sky. Partly, it refers to the spiritual realm. In the ancient mind, the two images were blended, and some people, such as modern atheists, often imagine that modern believers still function at that Bronze Age level of cognition. So, for example, there is the famous story of Soviet Premier Nikita Khrushchev scoffing that cosmonaut Yuri Gagarin had not seen God when he became the first human being to journey into outer space in 1961. And of course, there are those innocents today who bill themselves as New Atheists, pointing out to us childish believers that God is not an old man sitting on a cloud. The reply to this sort of confusion is that New Atheists really need to attempt to understand both the ancient and the modern religious mind a bit better.

What they would see, if they did make such an attempt, has been aptly described in the title of a book called *Before Philosophy*.[16] The point of the book is that, in many cases, the distinctions that Western man will make, subsequent to antiquity and sometimes well after the start of the Christian era, did not exist for many ancients. For instance, there were no hard and fast categories for science, art, magic, religion, philosophy, and math in remote antiquity because the universe was typically received as a *connected whole* rather than chopped up into academic fields of specialization. So, for instance, Pythagoras, whom we moderns are taught to regard strictly as a secular mathematician, did not see mathematics cut off from the spiritual realm but as emblematic of it. After all, what are the two places where you encounter things that are absolutely real and yet which are not composed of either matter or energy, nor do they exist in time or space? Answer: spirits and numerical values both have this strange quality. You can grasp the reality of "two-ness" without having two *things* in front of you. Mathematics runs through everything, holding things together in a colossal and elegant dance of equations, as though it were the language — or better still, the syntax — of God's creative speech. So Pythagoras saw no particular reason to quarantine his cogitations about numbers into the box called "mathematics," while keeping his musings about the transmigration of souls in a box called "religion." It was all one to him.

Similarly, the Babylonian Magi in the New Testament who studied the heavens saw no particular division between what we would later distinguish as astrology, astronomy, science, and religion. It was all one, all connected. Much the same idea was present in the minds of biblical writers. For instance, in Revelation 4 and 5, we meet the "four living creatures" — angelic beings St. John the Evangelist describes as looking like a lion, an ox, a man, and an eagle. These images, in turn, refer us back to the vision of Ezekiel 1, in which the prophet, in exile in Babylon some six centuries before John, sees an identical vision. But there's also strong evidence to link these four images to the constellations of the zodiac, according to biblical scholars like Michel Barnouin,[17] Austin Marsden Farrer, and David Chilton.[18] For (like all ancient peoples) the biblical writers indicate a high degree of familiarity with the constellations, with the exception that Scorpio was probably known to them as the Eagle. The four cherubim mentioned in Revelation 4:6-7 are very likely the middle signs in the four quarters of the zodiac: The lion is Leo, the ox is Taurus, the man is Aquarius, and the eagle corresponds to Scorpio. John lists them in counterclockwise order, backward around the zodiac.

This is not, however, an example of star worship on John's part any more than Matthew's Gospel is a tribute to the Babylonian astrology of the Magi. Rather, it's just another example of the common biblical understanding that the heavens, like all the rest of creation, are a sign made by God and pointing to God. In the words of Psalm 19:1, "The heavens are telling the glory of God." To the people of biblical times, the groupings of the stars are not random, for the simple reason that nothing in creation is random. Rather, they thought the macrocosm of creation showed the glory of God writ large across the heavens, just as the microcosm of the tabernacle and, later, the Temple showed it on a smaller, more intimate scale.[19] What we are seeing, in fact, is a sort of embryonic sacramentalism, whereby the invisible is made visible through the physical.

So it should be no surprise to us that John's star imagery borrows not from paganism but from Jewish Scripture, for the Jews did not consider the zodiac as a pagan thing, any more than they thought about walking around on two legs as a pagan thing. They treated the stars as part of the common patrimony of nature given to us by God and accorded them a sort of quasi-sacramental status as signs of the "heavenly host" of angels. Since the Jews didn't worship the stars or planets as gods, they saw them as signs of God at work in the heavenlies and ordering all creation.

In fact, in the Old Testament (Numbers 2), the arrangement of the twelve tribes of Israel around the tabernacle probably corresponded to the zodiac and its twelve signs. At least six ancient synagogues at Hammat Tiberias, Beit Alpha, Huseifa, Susiya, Naaran, and Sepphoris are decorated with the zodiac. The hope of the twelve tribes of the Chosen People was that Israel was the beginning of the new order of things, whose destiny and divine authorship were symbolized by the twelve constellations. Indeed, the link between the "heavenly host" ruled by Yahweh Sabaoth (the "Lord of hosts") and the nation of Israel is very strong, for the heavenly host, or army of angelic powers symbolized by the stars, is ruled over by the very same God who commands the armies of Israel, or the "earthly host." The earthly tabernacle was understood by Israelites to be a miniature of God's heavenly dwelling. Both were attended by the armies of the Lord, composed of the angels and the people of Israel.

So, for example, in Genesis 37:9, Jacob and his family are likened to the sun, moon, and twelve stars. The book of Judges also reflects the notion that the "heavenly host" of God and the earthly host of Israel are all members of the army of God. That's why Judges 5:20 celebrates the defeat of Jabin and his general Sisera by singing, "From heaven fought the stars, from their courses they fought against Sisera." Once again, the tendency of the ancient mind to see things as connected, rather than as separated, is in evidence. Heaven (in what we moderns call the "spiritual sense") and the heavens (meaning the skies above, whether full of puffy clouds or stars) were seen as connected. But it seldom occurred to the ancient mind to probe the nature of the connection or distinguish the spiritual reality from the thing symbolizing it. That mind saw the connectedness of things, and it saw something else — warfare, even in the heavenlies.

Let me give you some biblical passages to give you an idea of what I mean:

> For I am sure that neither death, nor life, nor angels, nor principalities, nor things present, nor things to come, nor powers, nor height, nor depth, nor anything else in all creation, will be able to separate us from the love of God in Christ Jesus our Lord. (Romans 8:38-39)

> For we are not contending against flesh and blood, but against the principalities, against the powers, against the world rulers of this present darkness, against the spiritual hosts of wickedness in the heavenly places. (Ephesians 6:12)

> He is the image of the invisible God, the first-born of all creation; for in him all things were created, in heaven and on earth, visible and invisible, whether thrones or dominions or principalities or authorities — all things were created through him and for him. (Colossians 1:15-16)

> He disarmed the principalities and powers and made a public example of them, triumphing over them in him. (Colossians 2:15)

> To me, though I am the very least of all the saints, this grace was given, to preach to the Gentiles the unsearchable riches of Christ, and to make all men see what is the plan of the mystery hidden for ages in God who created all things; that through the church the manifold wisdom of God might now be made known to the principalities and powers in the heavenly places. (Ephesians 3:8-10)

What's striking about all this, of course, is that even after we have distinguished between heaven-as-sky and heaven-as-spiritual-reality, Paul does not seem to share our modern-day image of heaven — or perhaps more precisely "the heavenlies" — as a particularly tranquil place. Nor does John, in his turbulent Revelation, which seems to summarize the early Christian picture of things by declaring flatly that "war arose in heaven" (Revelation 12:7). In short, the biblical vision of a heaven ruled by the Lord of hosts suggests that our modern picture of puffy clouds and nothing but peace is rather inadequate and that this may contribute mightily to our wrong notions of the life of prayer and phrases like "Thy will be done on earth, as it is in heaven."

Prayer is a great struggle, not a retreat into Nirvana. What Tradition has always maintained is that the reason for the struggle is threefold: the world, the flesh, and the devil. Different strains of modernity have different objections to this proposition. Many people, conditioned to think only in terms of the visible universe and the utterly unconditioned reality of God in eternity, find it incredible to believe that reality might have more than two floors. So they are startled by Scripture's "primitive" vision of a heavenly realm in which there is warfare and battle between the Lord of hosts and the "principalities and powers in the heavenly places" that Paul speaks of. Such folks are often also inclined to reject the notion of the only really trustworthy conspiracy theory in the world: namely, Paul's description of the "principalities and powers," the "world rulers of this present darkness," and the "spiritual hosts of wickedness in the heavenly places." For similar reasons, they don't know what to make of notions like the "prince of the power of the air" (Ephesians 2:2) or of Paul's strange remarks about being caught up to the "third heaven" (2 Corinthians 12:2). It has not occurred to most modern believers that there can be anything besides our physical universe, which is what "earth" refers to theologically, and "heaven," meaning "total union with God in Christ."

But, in fact, Scripture gives us every reason to think that "heaven" has another, unsuspected-by-moderns meaning in the minds of the biblical authors: namely, that instead of a simple two-story structure of earth below and heaven above, there is a sort of skyscraper of created orders and beings, which, while "supernatural" to us, are still creatures and infinitely inferior to God. And not all of these created spiritual beings are friendly to us or to God, judging from Paul's remarks. At the very minimum, there appears to be a pretty constant message, from the story of the Fall (where *something* was here before us to tempt us) to the Exodus (where God is making war on the gods of Egypt, and those gods try to fight back) to the contests of the Old Testament (where the prophets likewise make war on spiritual beings who aren't so much non-existent as "not God" — e.g., 1 Kings 18) to the Gospels (where Jesus is in open warfare with spiritual beings who can possess and inflict sundry harms on human beings — e.g., Mark 1:21-27) to Paul (who takes it for granted that the gods of the pagans are demons — e.g., 1 Corinthians 10:20-21).

The medieval period, taking this cue from Scripture's cryptic remarks, had great fun elaborating an angelology (and demonology) that one need not be persuaded is especially sound. At the same time, this habit of mind preserved something that modernity could really stand to recover: the recognition that prayer is a *battle* and that we really are involved with a creation that is much, much bigger than we realize: one that really does include powers, principalities, and sundry spiritual beings, both good and evil, beyond this visible creation. Moreover, it reinforces for us a realistic sense of our position in the world as creatures who are, by nature, lower than angels and yet, by grace, lifted far above them. That's the point of Paul's startling remark that "through the church the manifold wisdom of God might now be made known to the principalities and powers in the heavenly places" (Ephesians 3:10) and Peter's comment that even angels long to look into the mysteries which God is revealing through the Church (1 Peter 1:12).

This is not to say we are any great shakes, of course. Rather, it is to say that God has chosen to work out his purposes through the lowest and most undeserving of his creatures so that no creature can boast (1 Corinthians 1:18-31) — even the mighty thrones, dominations, principalities, and powers whom he has fashioned to serve him.

Augustine tells us:

> It would not be inconsistent with the truth to understand the words, "Thy will be done on earth, as it is in heaven," to mean: "in the Church as in our Lord Jesus Christ himself"; or "in the Bride who has been betrothed, just as in the Bridegroom who has accomplished the will of the Father."[20]

In short, Jesus, not some place in the clouds, is heaven. If you want to see how God's will is fulfilled "in heaven" so that you can imitate it here on earth, then don't wait around for a vision of angels in realms of glory and try to imitate that. Instead, look at Jesus. He is heaven on earth, and we must imitate him in the battle of prayer and obedience. In the incarnation of Jesus Christ, heaven joins earth to Jesus himself and brings the battle to the foe. He literally does the will of God on earth as it is in heaven because he *is* heaven come to earth.

In so doing, he prepares the way for that day when not just earth but even heaven will be freed from its wars and strife and be joined with the Blessed Trinity, not merely in a New Earth but a New Heaven as well (Revelation 21:1).

Chapter 7

GIVE US THIS DAY OUR DAILY BREAD

Most sane people never ask, "Did Michelangelo cause the statue of David, or was it his chisel? Did Shakespeare cause *Hamlet*, or was it his pen? Choose!"

But for some reason, when the subject turns to evolution, many fundamentalists, both atheist and Christian, completely forget that a thing can have primary and secondary causes. Instead, they start by demanding that we choose between God and nature, one or the other, as the sole cause of life on earth. The answer, from a Catholic perspective, is: "Why not both? God made me and used secondary causes called 'my ancestors' to do it. So why couldn't he have used a massive artillery of secondary causes stretching back 13 billion years to do it?"

Secondary causes do God's will all the time. Pigs serve God according to their piggy nature, rooting around in the mud and having a swine old time of it causing piglets. Dogs serve God according to their doggy nature, eating with gusto, adoring their masters, sniffing the daylights out of everything in scent, and causing puppies. Stars serve God's purposes according to their starry nature by burning brightly and, now and then, exploding and making heavier elements such as carbon, useful for building things like pigs and dogs and you and me. God made them that way, to his glory.

Of course, when it comes to those secondary causes called "human persons," since God made these particular causes to be rational animals in his own image and likeness, new dimensions enter in — dignity and free will. Treatment perfectly appropriate for pigs and dogs is inappropriate for men and women, which is why the former dislike being called swine and the latter dislike being called bitches. We are human beings, not beasts, and are entitled to be treated as such.

Because of our unique status in the created order, we humans have the duty and privilege of doing something no other animal can do: we can ask God for things. We can even ask for God to do things — often quite remarkable things — for *our* causality is unique. Pigs cause more pigs, and dogs more dogs. Both can cause stains on the carpet if you keep them in the house. But man alone can cause, not merely natural events, but even supernatural ones to happen, because he can ask God to move his hand and perform mighty works.

"Give us this day our daily bread" is the clause in the Our Father where Jesus sums up this paradox of our position before God as we enter into petitionary prayer. There are several things to note about it, the first being the marvel that it exists at all. Christians may not see this as clearly as non-Christians do, so let a former non-Christian point out what they take for granted.

Growing up, I was not baptized and never went to church. I had a curious scruple against petitionary prayer, not because I was an atheist (not enough faith for that), but because as a pagan with a cloudy reverence for the Unknown God, I considered it both the height of arrogance and emblematic of a sort of welfare-state mentality. I thought: "Why should God bother himself playing waiter and bellhop to insignificant specks who were constantly looking for handouts on this insignificant grain of sand orbiting a third-rate star on the rim of an unremarkable galaxy? He's got billions of such galaxies to juggle. So deal with it yourself and don't pester the Almighty with your stupid requests."

This rugged sort of libertarian theology, of course, eventually fell on hard times as I discovered things like "I am a creature who could not so much as exist without God actively willing it from nanosecond to nanosecond" and, more embarrassing still, "I am a wretched sinner who needs God's help, not only for my daily necessities, but still more because without his help I would be a monster, not a Jeffersonian paragon of the Free and Good Man at Home in Nature." So I discovered that petitionary prayer, while certainly not the highest form of prayer, is still good, and not merely permitted but commanded by our Lord. That such an infinite God could hear, much less lovingly answer, our prayers ought to astonish us.

Another thing I noticed was that Jesus' petitionary prayers have none of the sort of courtly embroidery that surrounds what we normally think of as "religious language." There is a matter-of-fact brevity to the Lord's Prayer that could almost be taken as rudeness if we didn't know this was the Son of God teaching us. Picture yourself at a family dinner where the teens look the adult in the eye and say, "Give me the bread," without so much as a "please." Yet this is the norm set out for us in the Lord's Prayer. No "please." No "O Great and Gracious God, if it is possible, though we are wretches who deserve nothing but death, of your ineffable kindness, we beg that you would stoop down and, from your endless bounty, give us a morsel of bread, and we will praise you forever for your goodness to us." Just a straightforward, "Give us this day our daily bread." It's a prayer of pure trust such as you only see from really small children who have not yet learned that some adults need to be truckled to, children who have completely internalized the fact that their father loves them and will give them what they need. It is, in a curious sense, the opposite of selfishness since, as the *Catechism* says:

> The trust of children who look to their Father for everything is beautiful. "He makes his sun rise on the evil and on the good, and sends rain on the just and on the unjust" (cf. Matthew 5:45). He gives to all the living "their food in due season" (Psalm 104:27). Jesus teaches us this petition, because it glorifies our Father by acknowledging how good he is, beyond all goodness. (CCC 2828)

Like the whole of the Our Father, this petition is made in the full awareness that prayer is always done in community. Just as we do not pray the *My* Father, so we do not pray, "Gimme this day my daily bread." Instead, we pray as members of the covenant community of Jesus, people who have not invented this stuff for themselves, nor figured it out on their own, but who have been graciously welcomed into the Body of Christ by God and by other members of the Body, without whom we would be completely lost.

By the same token, as we pray for "us" we pray on behalf of others who, likewise, need the help of our prayers, just as much as we depend on the prayers of others. Our request for daily bread goes up to heaven, not only on behalf of us and our loved ones but also for the Church around the world. Somewhere in Somalia, a child may well be getting a meal right now because you, sitting in Suburbia, USA, prayed, "Give *us* this day *our* daily bread." This is solidarity in action, in heaven, with the expectation, of course, that we shall likewise put it into practice "on earth, as it is in heaven." That is why the Christian tradition has always linked this prayer to concrete works of mercy such as feeding the hungry. To pray this prayer and ignore those in the world without the common necessities of life is to risk playing the wrong part in the parable of Lazarus and the Rich Man (Luke 16:19-31). Our unstable age tends to want to place a crazy emphasis on work versus prayer, as opposites, as though those who pray are exempt from feeding the hungry and those who do social activism don't need to pray. The sane Catholic balance is to pray as if everything depended on God and work as if everything depended on us.

At its most elemental level, of course, "Give us this day our daily bread" is a prayer asking God to meet our elementary bodily needs, including food, drink, shelter, medicine, work, love, etc. Christian prayer has great sympathy for those in need, but not so much for those praying out of mere renegade appetite. Contrary to the "health and wealth" prosperity Gospel preacher, the Gospel counsels have tended to radiate a general suspicion of hankering after more than you actually need.

This doesn't mean that we should offer "modest" petitionary prayers but rather that we should offer petitionary prayers which seek to glorify God rather than our own appetites. When the goal is God's glory, Jesus urges us to think big: "For truly, I say to you, if you have faith as a grain of mustard seed, you will say to this mountain, 'Move hence to yonder place,' and it will move; and nothing will be impossible to you" (Matthew 17:20).

When it comes to the whole "O Lord, won't you buy me a Mercedes-Benz" school of prayer, James sums up the general biblical attitude:

> What causes wars, and what causes fightings among you? Is it not your passions that are at war in your members? You desire and do not have; so you kill. And you covet and cannot obtain; so you fight and wage war. You do not have, because you do not ask. You ask and do not receive, because you ask wrongly, to spend it on your passions. (James 4:1-3)

Prayers prayed for the glory of God rather than for the delectation of our appetites can and do result in stunning acts of provision and grace from God. Whole religious orders in the Church, such as the Dominicans and the Sisters of Providence, have essentially functioned on the assumption that God will provide what is necessary, and they have achieved a global impact.

That said, at the end of the day, petitionary prayer is ultimately ordered toward our eternal good and not merely to our temporal good. The Jesus who taught us this prayer and told his followers that to feed the hungry is to feed him (Matthew 25:31-46) is the same Jesus who said, "Man shall not live by bread alone, but by every word that proceeds from the mouth of God" (Matthew 4:4). Therefore, the prayer for our daily bread is pregnant with significance in the Eucharistic tradition of the Church. As the *Catechism* says:

This petition, with the responsibility it involves, also applies to another hunger from which men are perishing: "Man does not live by bread alone, but . . . by every word that proceeds from the mouth of God" (Deuteronomy 8:3; Matthew 4:4), that is, by the Word he speaks and the Spirit he breathes forth. Christians must make every effort "to proclaim the good news to the poor." There is a famine on earth, "not a famine of bread, nor a thirst for water, but of hearing the words of the LORD" (Amos 8:11). For this reason the specifically Christian sense of this fourth petition concerns the Bread of Life: The Word of God accepted in faith, the Body of Christ received in the Eucharist (cf. John 6:26-58). (CCC 2835)

Hebrew (and its cognate Aramaic) is a language without degrees of emphasis. You don't say, "God is very, very holy." Instead, the way you emphasize is to *repeat*, for instance, saying, "Holy, holy, holy is the LORD of hosts" (Isaiah 6:3). In a similar way, the pedagogical style of the Hebraic teacher is to rhyme *ideas* rather than words. So, for instance, Jesus' teaching "Ask, and it will be given you; seek, and you will find; knock, and it will be opened to you" (Matthew 7:7).

Something like this is also going on in "Give us *this day* our *daily* bread." Strictly speaking, you could simply say, "Give us bread each day," but instead Jesus teaches us to emphasize our moment-by-moment dependence on God. Instead of some vast abstract theory about a God who inks a "once saved, always saved" contract with us and then leaves us alone to do as we please until whisking us off to heaven, this petition reminds us that we can make no lifetime guarantees of fidelity to God in his absence. Apart from him, says Jesus, we can do nothing (John 15:5). We are to live, day by day, in dependence on the day-by-day provision of God, with only the light sufficient to see the next step. Thus, and in no other way, do we learn humility.

One final tidbit about the petition "Give us this day our daily bread" is that the word translated as "daily" (*epiousios*) occurs nowhere else in the New Testament. The literal translation of the word is "super-essential" and is, quite consciously, meant to remind us of the fact that, particularly in the profoundly Eucharistic New Testament, "bread" never means merely "the stuff you eat that is made of flour." Rather, "bread" always has a Eucharistic connotation as well. This can be seen, for instance, in Luke's Gospel. The evangelist bookends the whole account with Christ's birth at Bethlehem ("House of Bread") and his being laid in manger (a feed box) at one end of the story while, at the other end, he tells us the tale of Christ's revelation on the Emmaus road when he took bread, gave thanks, broke it, and the eyes of the disciples were opened to see him. All through the Gospels, miracles involving bread and wine are directly connected to the source and summit of our faith — the Holy Eucharist. Likewise, then, the prayer for our daily bread is also a Eucharistic prayer. No wonder it is inseparable from the Eucharistic liturgy since here, supremely, we eat the true bread from heaven that Jesus came to give us in abundance.

There is a profound truth hidden in this. For with most petitionary prayer, there is no absolute guarantee that the answer is going to be yes. Indeed, one of the greatest tragedies that could befall the human race would be for God to grant every prayer ever offered him. So God does not promise us that we will never miss a meal. There are times we may pray for our daily bread and yet not get what we asked for. God sometimes says no. Hunger and even famine have stalked Christians at times, as they do the rest of our wretched race. Jesus fasted with us that we might, at times, fast with him and experience bodily hunger as one of the ways into his holy cross.

But there is one place where God has never, in all the history of the Church, said no to the petition "Give us this day our daily bread," and that is in the Holy Sacrifice of the Mass. There, every time the liturgy has been validly celebrated, God has sent his Spirit to transform mere earthly bread into the body, blood, soul, and divinity of Jesus Christ, the Bread of Life. Prayed in that context, this petition is, without any possible comparison, the prayer that God always answers with a resounding yes.

Chapter 8

AND FORGIVE US OUR TRESPASSES ...

When asked why he had become a Catholic, G. K. Chesterton famously replied, "To get rid of my sins."[21] The forgiveness of sins is the awesome gift Christ offers us, a gift so beautiful that words can scarcely express the glory of it. One of the most lovely things you can possibly experience is going to the Easter Vigil and watching the sheer joy of the newly baptized when, among the many other miracles that occur on that wonderful night, they emerge from the waters as new creations whose sins God will remember no more. It is a miracle so profound that fairy tales strain to capture the heartbreaking beauty of it with myths of the fountain of youth. Likewise, tragic stories communicate to us the dark side of the refusal of the gift with bitterly sad stories of people who, in their headstrong folly, get what they want, only to lose the love of their life forever.

That God himself gives us the petition "Forgive us our trespasses, as we forgive those who trespass against us" ought to startle us. After all, it places us in the odd position of the student studying for the finals who is handed a folder with all of the answers by the teacher himself. It's like going to court on a murder charge, having the defense counsel coach us on how to get a favorable verdict from the judge, and then having the defense counsel don robes and ascend the bench to hear our plea. It throws the whole picture of God as judge into a very odd light. Forgiveness is ours for the asking, saith the Lord. Just ask for it!

However, "asking for forgiveness" means we must really mean it. And the test of whether we mean it is bound up, as the *Catechism* says, with that pesky little word "as":

Now — and this is daunting — this outpouring of mercy cannot penetrate our hearts as long as we have not forgiven those who have trespassed against us. Love, like the Body of Christ, is indivisible; we cannot love the God we cannot see if we do not love the brother or sister we do see (cf. 1 John 4:20). In refusing to forgive our brothers and sisters, our hearts are closed and their hardness makes them impervious to the Father's merciful love; but in confessing our sins, our hearts are opened to his grace. (CCC 2840)

In short, once again, the Lord's Prayer is absolutely predicated on the fact that Christ's revelation is corporate and communal, not individualistic. Just as we pray, "*Our* Father," not "My Father," and pray, "Give *us* this day *our* daily bread," so we also pray, "Forgive *us* our trespasses, *as we forgive those who trespass against us*," not "Forgive me my trespasses, as I forgive those who sin against me."

The implications of this are enormous and account for why it has long been my conviction that the single most scandalous doctrine in Christian teaching is to be found right here — in the demand to forgive absolutely everybody for absolutely every sin he or she has committed against us.

Jesus seems to have anticipated something of the same thing, given that, of all the commentary he might have offered on the Our Father, the sole clause he focuses on is this one, precisely in order to hammer home how crucial is the command to forgive others if we expect to have any hope of forgiveness for ourselves. In Matthew, he tells us: "For if you forgive men their trespasses, your heavenly Father also will forgive you; but if you do not forgive men their trespasses, neither will your Father forgive your trespasses" (Matthew 6:14-15).

In Mark 11:25, he offers us even less wiggle room: "And whenever you stand praying, forgive, if you have *anything against any one*; so that your Father also who is in heaven may forgive you your trespasses" (emphasis added).

In short, Christ's test of whether we are really serious when we ask forgiveness for ourselves is whether we are really willing to extend it to others, regardless of whether they want it. This is a colossally hard saying, so over the centuries Christians have developed an impressive repertoire of strategies for avoiding, minimizing, evading, and explaining it away. Among them are the following:

- **Call "excusing" the same thing as "forgiving" and pat yourself on the back for it as the summit of Christian virtue.** Now excusing wrongs done to you is a fine thing and should be our first resort in treating others charitably. To paraphrase Mark Twain, never attribute to malice what can be sufficiently explained by stupidity (or some other less culpable cause like ignorance, clumsiness, or bad luck). When somebody steps on your toe accidentally, you are quite right to excuse him for it. He meant you no harm. But of course, as Jesus notes, even tax collectors and sinners can muster *that* much mercy. It's the emotional equivalent of lending and receiving back a couple of bucks for a cup of coffee. No actual forgiveness is taking place, merely simple justice. Until the excuses for offenses are exhausted, we haven't even *begun* the work of forgiveness. Because forgiveness is for sins — low-down, dirty, mean, intentional, nasty *sins* — not for mistakes. If you "forgive" somebody who steps on your toe accidentally, but not the SOB who stomps on it on purpose, you haven't forgiven at all.

- **Put a limit on the severity of the sin**, as in "I can forgive a little shoplifting. I was young once too. But I draw the line at out-and-out theft!" or "Every man has a wandering eye, but when a husband commits adultery, he commits the unforgivable!" The problem with this is that the measure you use will be the measure used on you. If you won't forgive mortal sin in others, don't expect any mercy for your own.

- **Put a number limit on forgiveness**, like "three strikes and you're out." Our Lord's remark on forgiveness, "I do not say to you seven times, but seventy times seven" (Matthew 18:22), is the obvious rejoinder here. If you've sinned more than three times yourself, it's highly advisable you extend the same mercy to others.

- **Call forgiveness "cheap grace."** This is the notion that if you don't go on hating that guy who ditched you, if you don't keep repeating to yourself every day the litany of wrongs your mother-in-law has done to you, if you don't cling to bitterness over that guy who took your job, then your enemy will have gotten away with it! The thought "I must not let them off the hook!" sums this up. But forgiveness does not equal passivity in the face of evil. It means releasing the evildoer into the hands of God's mercy, even as you finger him to the cops for his crime. A rape victim has the right and the duty to see to it that her attacker goes to jail with the help of her testimony. She likewise has the right and the duty to forgive that attacker, precisely so that he does not retain power over her for the rest of her life by robbing her of her happiness.

Related to this is another false notion arising from this bad understanding of forgiveness: the idea that stewing in rage is tantamount to "doing something about sin." I remember a woman I knew, incensed by the priest abuse scandal, telling me, "Love does not permit continued sin. I do not love an abusing priest or an enabling bishop by telling him, 'That's okay — I forgive you and God will forgive you,' when there is no reason to suspect he will repent and sin no more. He has demonstrated that he will do it again, if I let him off the hook."

The problem is that my friend was living in a complete fantasy world, imagining that cursing at a computer screen or TV would somehow affect the actions of bad bishops, abusive clergy, police, prosecutors, and so forth on the opposite side of the country. But of course, somebody swearing at her TV in Ohio over some sin committed by a priest in Boston is going to do absolutely nothing except corrode her own soul. Her refusal to let go of rage did not teach somebody a lesson, chasten a bad cleric, help the cops do their job, or comfort a victim. It just ate away at her own heart.

Related to this is another particularly silly argument that "Forgiveness cannot take place until we know the extent of what must be forgiven." The claim here is that if a sinner continues to sin, then we don't have to forgive him, since we allegedly can't forgive what he has not yet done or what is not yet known to have been done.

Rubbish. That is exactly backward from Christ's approach. He does not wait until our lives are over to decide whether or not he loves us. "God shows his love for us in that while we were yet sinners Christ died for us" (Romans 5:8). He commands us to do the same. That is what "love your enemies" means (Matthew 5:44). "Forgive, if you have anything against any one" (Mark 11:25) doesn't mean "Love people who pay back your emotional bank account by saying they are sorry and assuaging your rage." It means "Extend unconditional love and forgiveness to nasty people who despise you and want to harm you. Desire their happiness. Do not cultivate bitterness against them. Fight their evil actions, where necessary and possible, but do not will them ill."

Still another common dodge is to say, "God does not forgive impenitent sinners. Why should we be held to a higher standard than that to which God holds himself?" This clever retort sounds good, but it all hinges on what we mean by a "higher" standard. Obviously, no standard is "higher" than God's own standard in the sense of "better" or "more perfect." But if by "higher" you really mean "stricter," then there is a very sufficient answer to this question: "Because we're not God."

The sleight of hand at work here is the notion that God would never forbid us something he doesn't forbid himself. This is nonsense. We are commanded "Judge not" by the judge of the whole world. Why? Because we are not qualified to judge anybody and he is qualified to judge everybody. In other words, it is precisely *because* we are not God that we are commanded to forgive.

Still another excuse for refusing forgiveness goes this way: "The command to forgive is not unconditional, because if it were, a priest could not refuse absolution. Since, in some cases, the priest is supposed to refuse absolution, so can we refuse to forgive." This is, however, to confuse sacramental confession with the common Christian demand for forgiveness. Like it or not, the command "Whenever you stand praying, forgive, if you have anything against any one" (Mark 11:25) is unconditional, just as the command to love our enemies is. And it is coupled with the equally unconditional (and dire) assurance that "if you do not forgive men their trespasses, neither will your Father forgive your trespasses."

Pastors with a responsibility to govern the Church are given latitude by our Lord to exercise discretion in the dispensation of sacramental absolution ("If you forgive the sins of any, they are forgiven; if you retain the sins of any, they are retained" [John 21:23]) precisely because they act *in persona Christi*, and we laity do not. This is why the *Catechism* is really quite blunt:

> Christian prayer extends to the *forgiveness of enemies* (cf. Matthew 5:43-44), transfiguring the disciple by configuring him to his Master. Forgiveness is a high point of Christian prayer; only hearts attuned to God's compassion can receive the gift of prayer. Forgiveness also bears witness that, in our world, love is stronger than sin. The martyrs of yesterday and today bear this witness to Jesus. Forgiveness is the fundamental condition of the reconciliation of the children of God with their Father and of men with one another (cf. 2 Corinthians 5:18-21).[22] (CCC 2844, emphasis in original)

Enemies are not tearful penitents like the sinful woman who anointed Jesus' feet, or the sheepish Thomas saying, "My Lord and my God" (John 20:28), or the prodigal son or any of those gratifying sorts of people who make us feel so grandly magnanimous when they come crawling back to us saying, "I was sooooo wrong and you were sooooo right! Please forgive me!" Enemies are people who hurt us, who mean to go on hurting us, and who have not the slightest intention of saying, "I'm sorry." It is these people Jesus commands us to love, and as a corollary, it is these people to whom we are commanded to extend forgiveness.

Realizing this shocking truth, yet another escape route people sometimes explore is this: "I can forgive evils done against me personally, but I don't have to forgive, say, the 9/11 conspirators because they did not affect me personally. That's why it was so presumptuous of Pope John Paul II to pray a prayer of forgiveness for them. That is for the victims to do, not some pope sitting in Rome in the comfort of a papal palace! He has no idea how those victims suffered!"

The trick behind this evasion is to allow yourself to identify with the victims of a sin enough to hate their enemies, but to pretend that this act of identification does not likewise oblige you to forgive their enemies as it obliges them. Basic rule of thumb: If a sin done to a stranger arouses pity for the stranger and loathing for the one who committed the sin, then to that degree you are bound to forgive it as if it were done to you.

"But," we splutter desperately, "do you really think, for example, that Osama bin Laden was owed forgiveness?"

No. Nobody is *owed* forgiveness. Unconditional love is, by definition, undeserved. Grace is grace, not something we deserve.

So, sooner or later, we return to the granite fact that we are solemnly commanded by Jesus Christ himself to extend forgiveness to absolutely everybody who sins against us, whether they ever repent or not.

Why does he give this command? Two reasons:

1. We're not God.
2. We will destroy our lives and damn our souls if we don't.

Here's the deal. We can refuse to forgive (insert Impenitent Jerk's name here) till the day we die. The actual, practical, real-world result of this will be: (a) nothing happens to Impenitent Jerk as a result of our unforgiveness, and (b) we are consumed with bitterness.

It is simply false that clinging to unforgiveness will somehow empower us to *do what needs to be done.* This is like confusing idling your motor at 3,000 RPM with driving. Unforgiveness is a purely destructive waste of time. It is the ultimate Faustian rip-off, stealing our soul and giving us nothing in return. We not only commit the sin of usurping the place of God, but we also have no effect whatever on the sinner while we eat ourselves alive with pointless, utterly unproductive, and impotent rage. It's like drinking poison and expecting the other guy to die. The truly Christian thing is to act in whatever practical and just way we can and then hand the sinner over to God with the words, "I forgive that person in the name of Jesus Christ." It isn't easy — and even worse, it must be done thousands of times.

You may well ask, "Who then can be saved?" A reasonable question since, left to ourselves and our own strength, the answer is "No one." But as the Son of Man said, "With men this is impossible, but with God all things are possible" (Matthew 19:26). We are not left to our own strength, and we can ask the help of God's mighty Holy Spirit to empower us in the lifelong work of growing in forgiveness and mercy. This is what the awesome power of the sacraments (especially Reconciliation and Eucharist) is, in no small part, ordered toward helping us to do.

Forgiveness of that miserable swine who did that awful thing to you sounds like death — and so it is. But as with all Christian death, it ends not in the grave but in resurrection and ascension. The world is replete with examples of its awesome power when we see it, from John Paul II forgiving the man who shot him to Holocaust victim Corrie ten Boom forgiving the sadistic concentration-camp guard who sought her out after the war. That is how victims of sin are set free to start new and happy lives, liberated from the power of their victimizers.

One good way to start this process is by putting our own sufferings in perspective in the grand scheme of things. Jesus tells the parable of the Unmerciful Servant (Matthew 18:23-35) as a sort of capstone to his discourse on how the Church should conduct its affairs on a daily basis. The central point of the parable is that compared with what the king sacrifices in showing mercy to his servant, a guy who owed him millions of dollars, our day-to-day grievances against one another are usually pretty small beer. We who have not endured what Jesus endured can, among other things, find the help of the Spirit to forgive our Mickey Mouse trials in life and slowly build up the strength to forgive the big sins we have had to endure at the hands of others, just as we ask Jesus to forgive our great sins. The servant who asks forgiveness for his own Mount Everest of debt while denying it to the poor schmoe who owes him a couple of bucks is just not serious. If the servant is not serious about forgiveness, he shall receive mercy according to how serious his request really was — a dreadful prospect. The point is that, in the words of the *Catechism* (CCC 2843), "[i]t is not in our power not to feel or to forget an offense; but the heart that offers itself to the Holy Spirit turns injury into compassion and purifies the memory in transforming the hurt into intercession."

The bottom line and paradox of the mercy of God is that there is no limit or measure to it. Like the ocean, we cannot possibly exhaust it. But like the ocean, we can only get wet if we get in it. Merely looking at it or wishing to be wet will not do. So the smallest effort at extending mercy will be rewarded by our God, yet he will not rest until we are as immersed in and overflowing with mercy as he is. For God is, as a character in George MacDonald's novel put it, "easy to please as he's ill to saitisfee."[23] Take a step toward forgiving that guy who gave you a wedgie forty years ago, and all the angels in heaven will rejoice. But that will be because you have taken the first, not the last, step toward full union with the Blessed Trinity, "the source and criterion of truth in every relationship" (CCC 2845). God will never leave you where you are until you are as fully happy as he means you to be: full of the love, joy, peace — and mercy — of God.

Chapter 9

AND LEAD US NOT INTO TEMPTATION

One of the great consolations Christians have is that we worship a God who has himself wrestled with temptation. At the Last Judgment, we will face not an Olympian abstraction who breezed through on his looks and money, nor a severe and icy critic who eyes us coldly and says, "Why can't you just *not be tempted*, like me!" but by a man who himself has faced and struggled through every temptation the world ever had to throw at our miserable species. God, it is true, asks a lot from us, and I, for one, have to admit that I sometimes resent it. But the fact remains that he doesn't ask anything of us to which he hasn't subjected himself. Hunger, thirst, misunderstanding, rejection, bitter hate, betrayal, torture, and death are all things he has faced, right along with the accompanying temptations to selfishness, self-pity, pride, lust, resentment, grudges, vengefulness, bitterness, and despair. And the temptations he faced occurred, not by accident, but by his own divine plan. Before he begins his mission, Jesus is described by Mark as being "driven" into the wilderness by the Spirit to be tempted by the devil. He fought and beat all of the temptations, and he tells us he will give us his Spirit in order that we may do likewise.

It is notable that the *Catechism* tells us (CCC 2846) that this petition against temptation "goes to the root of the preceding one" (i.e., "Forgive us our trespasses, as we forgive those who trespass against us"). Partly, that's because temptation is where sin is conceived, but also it is because perhaps the greatest temptation we feel in this life is the temptation to refuse forgiveness to others. After all, forgiveness is, by definition, for people who don't deserve it, since they really sinned against us and we really are their victims.

Because of this, we can feel an enormous temptation to "stand on our rights," instead of standing on the grace of Christ. Like the proud ghost in C. S. Lewis' wonderful little book *The Great Divorce*, we want to say, especially when we are really wronged, "I only want my rights, I'm not asking for anybody's bleeding charity." To which our guardian angel replies in Lewis' immortal words: "Then do. At once. Ask for the Bleeding Charity."[24]

It is curious that we pray to God, who has already put himself through hell to win us our salvation, to "lead us not into temptation." It seems as odd as asking a lifeguard not to deliberately drown us. Why on earth are we asking God not to do what he would never ever do? Part of the problem is that the Greek contains more ideas than can be adequately rendered in English. The *Catechism* tells us, "It is difficult to translate the Greek verb used by a single English word: the Greek means both 'do not allow us to enter into temptation' and 'do not let us yield to temptation' (cf. Matthew 26:41)" (CCC 2846).

Jesus is not teaching us that we worship a capricious deity who might suddenly take an irrational dislike to us, herd us into temptation, and try to damn us for fun. He is teaching us to worship his Father, the God of Israel, who "cannot be tempted with evil and he himself tempts no one" (James 1:13). God is absolutely consistent and is not about to suddenly and whimsically betray us like a fairy or sprite in some pagan myth. He is not perverse and mercurial. His purpose is from age to age. He means to set us free from sin, death, and the devil. But part of his purpose can only be fulfilled with our cooperation. So just as we ask the Father to give us what is good, so we ask him to protect us from temptation by helping us to avoid and escape it.

And, brother, do we need the help! We want to turn salvation into a legal game in which we seek, not to love the Lord with all our heart, mind, soul, and strength, but rather to see how much we can get away with and, as the saying goes, "still be saved." We have numerous elaborate strategies for attempting to offer as little of ourselves as we can to God, while trying not to appear as though we are basically seeking our own way. We see this in the sort of questioning that asks things like "How far can I go with my girl-friend before it's technically, you know, 'fornication'?" The very question reveals a corrupt will and intellect before the sin has even been technically, you know, committed. In the final analysis, it boils down to not-yet-converted Augustine's prayer, "Lord, make me chaste, but not yet!"[25] And we see the identical pattern with whatever other favorite sin we are trying to sidle up to.

So we are taught to ask God to guard us from the way that leads to sin for the same reason we ask him for our daily bread: because grace is as necessary for our spiritual life as bread is for our physical life. We are locked in combat between the flesh and the spirit, and we need all the help we can get to know how to discern what God is doing with us in the middle of this war zone. As Paul puts it:

> For you were called to freedom, brethren; only do not use your freedom as an opportunity for the flesh, but through love be servants of one another. For the whole law is fulfilled in one word, "You shall love your neighbor as yourself." But if you bite and devour one another take heed that you are not consumed by one another.
>
> But I say, walk by the Spirit, and do not gratify the desires of the flesh. For the desires of the flesh are against the Spirit, and the desires of the Spirit are against the flesh; for these are opposed to each other, to prevent you from doing what you would. But if you are led by the Spirit you are not under the law. Now the works of the flesh are plain: for-nication, impurity, licentiousness, idolatry, sorcery, enmity, strife, jealousy, anger, selfishness, dissension, party spirit, envy, drunkenness, carousing, and the like. I warn you, as I warned you before, that those who do such things shall not inherit the kingdom of God. But the fruit of the Spirit

is love, joy, peace, patience, kindness, goodness, faithfulness, gentleness, self-control; against such there is no law. And those who belong to Christ Jesus have crucified the flesh with its passions and desires.

If we live by the Spirit, let us also walk by the Spirit. Let us have no self-conceit, no provoking of one another, no envy of one another. (Galatians 5:13-26)

Satan's temptation, of course, always consists of using some good thing God has made and trying to lure us into loving it in a disordered way. No fish bites a bare hook. It's always wrapped in a juicy worm that is, like the apple in the Garden of Eden, tasty-looking both to our appetite and to our pride. But the hook is still death. This is why Paul tells us that Satan appears as an "angel of light" (2 Corinthians 11:14). The mark of the world, the flesh, and the devil is that we are told to seek some good (it matters not what) by rejecting what God has commanded. To break this ancient habit, it is necessary that God permits us to face trials, even as he teaches us to avoid temptation — and to learn to tell the difference.

Therefore, the *Catechism* tells us:

The Holy Spirit makes us *discern* between trials, which are necessary for the growth of the inner man (cf. Luke 8:13-15; Acts 14:22; Romans 5:3-5; 2 Timothy 3:12), and temptation, which leads to sin and death (cf. James 1:14-15). We must also discern between being tempted and consenting to temptation. Finally, discernment unmasks the lie of temptation, whose object appears to be good, a "delight to the eyes" and desirable (cf. Genesis 3:6), when in reality its fruit is death.

God does not want to impose the good, but wants free beings. . . . There is a certain usefulness to temptation. No one but God knows what our soul has received from him, not even we ourselves. But temptation reveals it in order to teach us to know ourselves, and in this way we discover our evil inclinations and are obliged to give thanks for the goods that temptation has revealed to us.[26] (CCC 2847)

One thing to note about temptation is that when we aren't actively courting it, we're facing, not sin, but *concupiscence*. Sadly, this term is one that has fallen into disuse in contemporary culture, leading to the tendency to conflate temptation with sin itself. A pattern of thought that afflicts many believers — and one that the devil, the accuser of the brethren, loves — is, "If I were truly a Christian, I wouldn't be having these thoughts and feelings at all." But this is not so. Temptation only sprouts into the weed of sin when we water it with consent of the will. That is why the Church speaks of concupiscence, not as sin, but as the "tinder for sin" when she teaches:

> Yet certain temporal consequences of sin remain in the baptized, such as suffering, illness, death, and such frailties inherent in life as weaknesses of character, and so on, as well as an inclination to sin that Tradition calls *concupiscence*, or metaphorically, "the tinder for sin" (*fomes peccati*); since concupiscence "is left for us to wrestle with, it cannot harm those who do not consent but manfully resist it by the grace of Jesus Christ."[27] Indeed, "an athlete is not crowned unless he competes according to the rules" (2 Timothy 2:5). (CCC 1264, emphasis in original)

To vary the metaphor, think of it this way: Original sin is like a birth defect. It's not so much a thing as the lack of something; a hole in our souls where God was supposed to be. Our first parents, in losing the life of God in their souls, lost it for us, so we are born without something that ought to be there — just as, for instance, a baby might be born with a missing heart valve. In Baptism, the life of God is given to us so that we can "walk with Christ" (cf. 1 John

2:6) — just as heart surgery for an otherwise fatal defect might save a child's life, yet leave him with a weakened constitution that easily tires. In the same way, we are healed from the death-dealing effects of original sin but still must grapple with a weakened will, a darkened intellect, and disordered appetites caused by that severe blow to our God-given human nature. None of these things are sinful by themselves, and in fact, they are the field of battle on which we live out our fidelity to Christ.

Indeed, it is precisely because concupiscence is *not* sin that God sees our struggle to overcome temptation, not as a revelation of how rotten we are at heart, but as the glorious battlefield upon which we grow in virtue, courage, and grace. I once had a conversation with a man who had struggled for years with homosexual temptation. He was married and had been a faithful husband and father, but he feared that his temptation revealed how sinful he really was. I told him what the Church taught about concupiscence and that the first thing he needed to know was that his Father in heaven was proud of him and said, "Well done, good and faithful servant." He had fought the good fight and loved his wife and family by the power of grace. He burst into tears. Nobody had ever told him about concupiscence. He had been taught that temptation told us who we "really" are and had lived for years with the burden of supposing God was constantly angry at him.

The truth is that Jesus is the revelation of who we really are. He, not sin, is the final word about the human person. Therefore, Paul tells us, "If we live by the Spirit, let us also walk by the Spirit" (Galatians 5:25). Note that Paul does not say, "If you give in to temptation, that proves you aren't really a Christian." That's why he tells a Corinthian Church that is positively riddled with sinful members, "Do you not know that the unrighteous will not inherit the kingdom of God? Do not be deceived; neither the immoral, nor idolaters, nor adulterers, nor homosexuals, nor thieves, nor the greedy, nor drunkards, nor revilers, nor robbers will inherit the kingdom of God. And such were some of you. But you were washed, you were sanctified, you were justified in the name of the Lord Jesus Christ and in the Spirit of our God" (1 Corinthians 6:9-11).

Paul, aware of the possibility of the radical misuse of our freedom, warns of the real possibility of damnation for his flock, but does not enter into the stupid game of attempting to claim that baptized people who sin, even gravely, are "not really Christians." Instead, he accepts the reality that they are, at least for the moment, *bad* Christians, exhorts them to become what they are, and reminds them of what that is. He does not say, "You pretended to be washed, sanctified, and justified." He takes it for granted that they were and demands that they conform their lives to the truth of what Christ has revealed in them through the sacraments.

The mystery here is that the sacraments are grace, not magic. They do not cancel our free will. Paul, of course, realizes that we will fail and fall, but that when we do, Christ's will is to forgive and heal and call us back to repentance once again, because he, not sin, is the final word about who we are. Note as well that, instead of concluding from this that he does not need to bother rebuking the wayward Corinthians because it will all turn out well in the end, Paul sees it as his duty to warn them that if they do not repent, they will not see the Kingdom of God. In short, he understands that just as "give us this day our daily bread" implies a duty to feed the hungry, so "lead us not into temptation" implies a duty to strengthen, encourage, and where necessary, warn and rebuke those who are struggling in the battle with temptation.

One of the great lessons the saints teach us is that the battle with sin is the hardest and longest battle there is. This is not a discovery of the New Testament saints but was already old news in the Old Testament. That's why the book of Proverbs tells us, "He who is slow to anger is better than the mighty, and he who rules his spirit than he who takes a city" (Proverbs 16:32). This imagery informs the New Testament as well when Paul tells us:

Finally, be strong in the Lord and in the strength of his might. Put on the whole armor of God, that you may be able to stand against the wiles of the devil. For we are not contending against flesh and blood, but against the principalities, against the powers, against the world rulers of this present darkness, against the spiritual hosts of wickedness in the heavenly places. Therefore take the whole armor of God, that you may be able to withstand in the evil day, and having done all, to stand. Stand therefore, having girded your loins with truth, and having put on the breastplate of righteousness, and having shod your feet with the equipment of the gospel of peace; besides all these, taking the shield of faith, with which you can quench all the flaming darts of the evil one. And take the helmet of salvation, and the sword of the Spirit, which is the word of God. (Ephesians 6:10-17)

The only weapon that will ultimately carry us through this battle to victory is prayer, with our eyes wide open, vigilant, and alert. This is how Jesus himself defeated the tempter, and it is why he calls us to "watch and pray" (Matthew 26:41). We are not to live in fear of the enemy or in an endless navel-gazing search for our own faults. We are instead to live as Christ did, with our eyes fixed on the Father and on the prize to which he called us when he prayed for us to the Father, "Keep them in thy name" (John 17:11). Only by such vigilant prayer can we overcome the enemy of our souls.

Chapter 10

BUT DELIVER US FROM EVIL

Years ago, I heard a Pentecostal pastor in Spokane talking about a time he and some other local nondenominational pastors had been asked by a family they knew to come and pray for their granny, who, her family said, "had an evil spirit." One of the pastors was of a more modern attitude — the sort that fancies itself "open-minded" by closing itself off from the very possibility of the supernatural ever actually occurring. He somehow found himself invited to this meeting of pastors who were going to this family's house, to pray for Granny. The modernist pastor reluctantly agreed and joined the circle as they gathered round Granny and began to ask God to intervene on her behalf.

The doubting pastor happened to have taken up a position right behind Granny, perhaps due to his reluctance to look at her face during what he considered to be a hugely superstitious bit of medieval hocus-pocus. Granny submitted to the prayer, but as it went on she began to act oddly and, quite suddenly, reached behind her (over her shoulders), seized the doubting pastor, and lifted him clean off the ground. "That kind of thing changes your theology," observed the Pentecostal pastor drily.

There are basically two approaches to the Church's teaching concerning the fact of the supernatural. One is the approach of the so-called rationalist materialist, who simply rejects it all because it doesn't fit into his philosophical system. This is called, in our culture, the open-minded pursuit of truth wherever the facts may lead. It is the great stick used by the New Atheists to beat ignorant obscurantist theists, especially those superstitious papists like Thomas Aquinas, Louis Pasteur, Gregor Mendel, and Father Georges Lemaitre, who — when they aren't conducting fearless philosophical inquiries, pioneering historic medical research, inventing the science of genetics, and formulating the Big Bang theory to revolutionize the world of physics and cosmology — fear science and rational inquiry.

This approach is all the rage in our era of unreason. To the question "Does the supernatural exist?" our highly rationalist age typically replies through the organs of media with the sort of investigative curiosity that typifies this exchange between Richard Dawkins, professional atheist and author of *The God Delusion*, and Hugh Hewitt, an American law professor, talk-show host, and Christian:[28]

> Dawkins: Okay, do you believe Jesus turned water into wine?
> Hewitt: Yes.
> Dawkins: You seriously do?
> Hewitt: Yes.
> Dawkins: You actually think that Jesus got water, and made all those molecules turn into wine?
> Hewitt: Yes.
> Dawkins: My God.

And so some people become hard-boiled materialists who believe in neither God nor the devil, shutting themselves up tight as a drum against the influence of God (who respects our freedom) but remaining, alas, wide open to the influence of the devil (who does not). For disbelieving in the devil does not make him go away, as the great atheist regimes of Stalin, Mao, and Pol Pot attest with an ocean of blood.

The other approach is that of the Catholic who says, "There are more things in heaven and earth than are dreamt of in your philosophy,"[29] and who, accordingly, admits the possibility that there may be something in tales of the supernatural. He does not instantly credit them as true, of course, but is open to investigation and, if the facts point to the reality of such tales, to accepting them as factual.

Chesterton sums this approach up quite nicely in *Orthodoxy*, when he replies to the knee-jerk rationalist rejection of miracles:

> It is we Christians who accept all actual evidence — it is you rationalists who refuse actual evidence being constrained to do so by your creed. But I am not constrained by any creed in the matter, and looking impartially into certain miracles of mediaeval and modern times, I have come to the conclusion that they occurred.[30]

The disbeliever in the devil, like the disbeliever in God, has no facts or evidence to go on in support of his denial, merely bigotry and a profoundly unreflective arrogance. Indeed, in the case of the devil, the mere skeptic who worships the intellect rather than using it is in an even dicier position than normal. With God, you at least have the fig leaf of the problem of evil to lend a cast of hard thought to your breezy skepticism masquerading as rationalism. Every time something suggests the ominous possibility that You Know Who actually exists and is good, you can always trot out your favorite Horrible and say, "Oh yeah? Would a good God permit *this*?"

But there's not much point in asking, "If the devil exists, why does he allow bad things to happen?" So you have to more or less shout the whole subject down, as Dawkins shouts Hewitt down, and simply never ask yourself if there is any solid testimony to the existence of supernatural evil. The motto of the ingrained skeptic is "Don't look," because looking could engender awkward questions.

This sort of intellectual contraception is one of the curious marks of our age, which avoids ultimates, whether of good or evil. So, for instance, oceans of ink are spent raising Darwin's standard as the definitive disproof of the existence of God, using the approved Scooby Doo method of debunking: "That wasn't a supernatural agency at work. That was just Old Mister Higgins in a bedsheet!" By this method, atheistic naturalists have, for years now, imagined that something has been "explained" when we are told that the laws of nature are so written that hydrogen is a thing which, given sufficient time, just naturally turns into Angelina Jolie. Nobody seems to find it remarkable that there is any hydrogen at all, much less that it "has" to behave as it does and that all the other physical laws are ordered to demand what they demand of time, space, matter, and energy. Nor does anybody find it remarkable that all this is intelligible to us. It all reminds me of a child who thinks he has "explained" a computer by understanding that when you press "a," the letter "a" appears on the screen. Just as the child lacks the deep curiosity to wonder, "Why is there a computer at all?" so the rationalist lacks the deep curiosity to wonder why there is anything at all, especially anything that is so manifestly contingent as our universe is.

You find secularists seriously imagining they've resolved the mystery of existence by quipping, "Who made me? My mother and father made me!" This is radical incuriosity. (Give me an ignorant medieval like Thomas Aquinas any day.) This radical incuriosity is nowhere more evident than in the rationalist who simply can't be bothered to look at things like the supernatural, whether Fátima or certain aspects of supernatural evil, and ask, "What do these things mean?" Typically, the best you can expect from our New Atheist Paladins of Reason and Science will be the old "Some claims of the supernatural are fraudulent, therefore all are" shtick.

In contrast is the friend I knew years ago who was an average sort of Western Washingtonian secularist but who was not afraid of "big questions." She once had a dream in which she met a vampire and, oddly, she found that, in the dream, she was relieved because her encounter with supernatural evil opened the possibility of supernatural goodness as well. During the dream, she reasoned, not without merit, that if there is supernatural evil, there has to be a good supernatural God too and that the whole secular project was basically a childish attempt to clamp one's eyes shut, rather than look at the terrifying immensity of the universe in which we live.

Of course, this was only a dream, but it reflects something that is quite real in the history of the Church: the confrontation between Christ and Satan is something that has had no small influence on the missionary activity of the Church. People come to Christ, at least in part, because he breaks the chains of evil that are destroying their lives. We see this already in the New Testament itself, when Jesus exorcises various people, or heals them, or otherwise liberates them from evil, and they become his followers as a result (e.g., Mark 5:1-20). As the pastor said, "That sort of thing changes your theology." The blind man Jesus healed becomes a follower of Jesus, not because somebody offered him a diagram of the Trinity or a theory about justification by grace through faith, but because there was one thing he knew for certain: "I was blind, now I see" (John 9:25).

The mission work of the Church down through the ages has offered something very similar. While the Church does not go looking for demons under every rug, she is, as Paul was, "not ignorant of his designs" (2 Corinthians 2:11), and has always preserved, in her liturgical life, her catechesis, and in the lives of her saints, the awareness that demonic powers are real and that we are engaged in a war that involves more than the merely human.

The only reply modernity has to this is empty claptrap like "But this is the twenty-first century!" One might just as well say, "But this is Tuesday!" It does not alter the fact that the Church, following Jesus, has always taught that there exist angelic beings (i.e., incorporeal rational beings created by God) who have abused their free will and made themselves enemies of God and of his creatures. There's no conceivable way science can have anything to say against that proposition, and there is plenty in our history, as well as in revelation, to support it, not only reaching back to the roots of the Christian tradition and its numerous accounts of exorcism, but even further back to the story of the Fall and of the mysterious dark presence who is already in the garden before Adam and Eve get there.

Jesus, of course, takes the devil for granted as a fact, as do his apostles. As the *Catechism* reminds us, the devil is:

"A murderer from the beginning, . . . a liar and the father of lies," Satan is "the deceiver of the whole world" (John 8:44; Revelation 12:9). Through him sin and death entered the world and by his definitive defeat all creation will be "freed from the corruption of sin and death."[31] Now "we know that anyone born of God does not sin, but He who was born of God keeps him, and the evil one does not touch him. We know that we are of God, and the whole world is in the power of the evil one" (1 John 5:18-19). (CCC 2852)

In the Christian tradition, evil is therefore more than merely misfortune or misunderstanding. It is not an illusion. It is real and, when it comes to that sort of manifestation of evil we call "sin," it is paradoxically personal and depersonalizing. Consider the great icon of evil in our time: the Nazi slaughter of the Jews. This act of barbarism required something no beast was capable of: extreme and prodigious amounts of organization, foresight, rational planning, and careful thought. It was, in a word, something only persons, not animals, could have achieved. Yet the whole point and effect of the thing was to reduce human beings to numbers and, ultimately, to ashes. The devil's work always has this creepy quality to it, because in sin both angels and men are using all the gifts God gives them to *assert their nothingness*, as Augustine puts it. Part of the lust of the demons is what C. S. Lewis describes as the aggressive desire to "*extend* Hell — to bring it bodily, if they could, into Heaven."[32]

Of course, hell cannot harm God in the slightest. So hell does what all cowards do; it attacks those whom God loves. That would be us, as well as the rest of the created order wherever possible. This is the sum of the Christian picture concerning our relationship with the forces of darkness. They hate God, us, and even themselves, since they owe their existence entirely to God and are utterly dependent upon him for what goods they still retain, such as existence, power, and will. The drama of our existence is carried out in the strange arena of a created order in which God permits such beings to act, within limits, and permits us to resist or succumb to their lies as we choose.

That's a vision of reality that is markedly more luminous and frighteningly darker than we generally care to face. Our radically incurious and timid culture of secularism makes a careful study of thinking about it as little as possible, all while carrying on the ridiculous charade of prattling about "freedom" versus the supposed restrictions that an evil theocratic Church is just about to impose on us all. But in fact, our culture wants nothing to do with real freedom. It wants comfort at all costs and does not want to contemplate for a second that God has chosen to allow us to live in a *very* dangerous world, where our choices have wide-ranging and eternal consequences. Just how dangerous may be seen in the story of what happened to God himself when he became man. A universe where devils and men are free to conspire to visit the horrors of crucifixion on the Creator of the universe is not a universe where we lack freedom. It is a universe where we face such terrifying and prodigious freedom that we are constantly inventing foolish little systems of order to try to rein in our radical capacity for evil.

Jesus' response to the radical capacity for evil of fallen angels and their human stooges is, first and foremost, prayer. On at least one occasion, he speaks of prayer as the big gun against the devil, instructing his disciples, who had failed to cast out a demon, that "this kind cannot be driven out by anything but prayer and fasting" (Mark 9:29). When was the last time you saw Christians fighting other obvious evils in this world by this means? For us, prayer is often the last, not the first resort. It would be a striking change indeed if our culture first went to prayer instead of to court, to war, or to fisticuffs. But when this is actually recommended while the blood is up and everybody is in a frenzy of war fever, those who recommend prayer as the first option tend to get dismissed as unrealistic, pious wimps who don't understand what it takes to oppose "real evil." Jesus would politely dissent from the view that demons don't constitute "real evil."

At the opposite extreme from the materialist skeptic is the person who believes in the devil — and takes too keen an interest in him. People can poison their souls with Satanism, the occult, and the worship of devils. Just as you can err by foolishly rejecting any belief in the devil at all, so you can also "believe in" the devil too much by cultivating the incredibly dangerous notion that you can ride the tiger by trying to "call spirits from the vasty deep."[33] This may strike those of a secular cast of mind as ridiculous and lurid, but it is worth noting that there is nothing in human history that particularly forbids us from supposing that a certain percentage of the population is drawn to the ridiculous, the lurid, and the occult. Certainly, there have arisen, from time to time, groups of people who embrace the notion that they can do what they themselves know to be gravely evil in order to achieve some good result, usually with the excuse that they are being "realistic" and "practical." Chesterton gets at this mind-set quite accurately when he writes in *The Everlasting Man* of the monstrous practices that have arisen from time to time in various decaying civilizations:

> Sooner or later a man deliberately sets himself to do the most disgusting thing he can think of. It is felt that the extreme of evil will extort a sort of attention or answer from the evil powers under the surface of the world. This is the meaning of most of the cannibalism in the world. For most cannibalism is not a primitive or even a bestial habit. It is artificial and even artistic, a sort of art for art's sake. Men do not do it because they do not think it horrible; but, on the contrary, because they do think it horrible. They wish, in the most literal sense, to sup on horrors. That is why it is often found that rude races like the Australian natives are not cannibals; while much more refined and intelligent races, like the New Zealand Maories, occasionally are. They are refined and

94

intelligent enough to indulge sometimes in a self-conscious diabolism. But if we could understand their minds, or even really understand their language, we should probably find that they were not acting as ignorant, that is as innocent cannibals. They are not doing it because they do not think it wrong, but precisely because they do think it wrong.[34]

Such embraces of evil do not always have an explicit occult cast to them. Sometimes we coat them with a scientific or *realpolitik* veneer as we relish the frisson of evil we are embracing for the sake of "realism." Quite often, we wrap the embrace of evil in the language of "courage" and tell ourselves we are being *brave* in our choice to do evil "for a good cause." So, for instance, Heinrich Himmler, in a secret speech given to SS troops carrying out the Holocaust, invokes precisely the language of brave, silent courage to describe the hardness of heart and painful searing of conscience committed by those carrying out the unspeakable slaughter "for the glory of the Fatherland":

> Most of you will know what it means when 100 bodies lie together, when there are 500, or when there are 1,000. And to have seen this through, and — with the exception of human weaknesses — to have remained decent, has made us hard and is a page of glory never mentioned and never to be mentioned.[35]

But no matter how loudly the mortal sinner lies to himself, there remain things we can't not know — which is why Himmler found it necessary to give the speech in order to silence the screaming consciences of his murdering goons. In the end, we still know that we are saying, "Let us do evil that good may come of it," whether the evil we happen to be embracing is murder, theft, adultery, torture, genocide, abortion, or anything else the devil delights in. Any of these sins will damn us, just so long as we go on explaining to God why he is hopelessly unrealistic and we are, in our pride, right to commit them. Of course, all these sins can, like billions of others, be forgiven if we simply repent of them and ask for the Mercy.

There is also another way of "believing in" the devil that has an odd affinity with direct dabbling in the occult. This is the paranoid way that some Christians can take with "spiritual warfare," which is actually a sort of terrified fascination with the devil that can supplant the worship of God. I have known Christians whose every waking hour was spent studying the darkness, "researching" the occult, and consuming hours, days, months, and years feverishly "making connections" between this and that feared occultic quack or movement, all in the barren and fruitless notion that they were somehow doing some good and not merely feeding an endless paranoid appetite for conspiracy. I have watched as such Christians have imprisoned their lives in little psychic hells, in which no one could be trusted, the devil lurked behind every good thing (including the Mass itself), and the universe appeared to them to be barren of God. The problem lay, not in God's absence, but with their persistent and stubborn choice to give Satan the glory by devoting all their waking thought to fearing him instead of loving God. It is a tragic choice, but one that we can all make in our own ways, whenever we opt to give fear, anger, doubt, and suspicion pride of place in our hearts. The irony is that Satan is quite as happy with those who neglect obedience to God in order to sup on the fear of devils as he is with those who dabble in the occult. In the end, it comes down to the same thing: prioritizing the amount of time you spend focusing on the devil over the amount you spend focusing on God. The point is to distract you from God. If that is accomplished by devil-fearing rather than devil-worshiping, Old Scratch doesn't care, just as long as it's not God-loving.

In contrast to all this is the healthy way of "believing in" Satan: namely, to accept his existence as part of the way the world is, much the way you accept the fact of AIDS, earthquakes, and bee stings, while taking care to avoid or minimize their danger.

There's no use crying over it or curling up in a helpless ball about it. Best to get on with life and follow Jesus by being aware of the devil's schemes so that when he attacks, you are not blindsided. But don't obsess about it either. Recall that "he who is in you is greater than he who is in the world" (1 John 4:4), and get on with the life of being a disciple of Jesus.

This is why "Deliver us from evil" is the last, not the first, of the petitions in the Our Father. It is suggestive of the place that fear of the devil should have in our lives. On the one hand, we should be aware that, apart from grace, we are not adequate to deal with the "prince of this world." That's why it's a petition in the Our Father. As the song says,

> For still our ancient foe
> doth seek to work us woe;
> his craft and power are great,
> and armed with cruel hate,
> on earth is not his equal.
>
> Did we in our own strength confide,
> our striving would be losing;
> were not the right man on our side,
> the man of God's own choosing.[36]

The "man of God's own choosing" is not you, empowered by your sense of self-worth. It is not Buffy the Vampire Slayer, who overcomes evil through girl power and the affirmation of her circle of friends. It is not any of the heroes of pop culture, who invariably look deep within themselves at their darkest hour and find that they have what it takes to be heroes. It is not anybody in Millennial America, filled with the notion that, with faith in the goodness of the American people, democratic capitalism, sufficient firepower, and therapeutic moralistic deism, we shall prevail.

That man is Jesus Christ, and him only. To be sure, by grace, we can participate in his glorious humanity and, by the Spirit, find the strength within to overcome evil — but only by grace, not because of our native and intrinsic wonderfulness. That is why Jesus teaches us to pray to God the Father, through him, to deliver us from evil — because we cannot deliver ourselves, whatever Yankee myths about Daniel Webster outwitting the devil we may have been taught. Apart from Jesus Christ, we can do nothing (John 15:5).

That said, however, the Christian and Catholic tradition is surprisingly lighthearted about the devil, whom medieval piety breezily called an ass and the ape of God. This attitude is right there in the apostolic DNA, when Paul tells us that Jesus "disarmed the principalities and powers and made a public example of them, triumphing over them in him" (Colossians 2:15). The Catholic tradition concerning the devil tends toward taking him seriously, but holding him lightly. It is the confidence of a tradition founded on the belief that the worst thing that could ever conceivably happen is not in some future apocalypse but in the past. After all, the worst thing that could ever happen is the murder of God, and God has already been murdered in the most brutal way possible. Yet this monstrous crime only served to bring about the greatest blessing God has ever wrought: the destruction of death and our incorporation into the life of the Blessed Trinity. Having wrought such an epic fail, the devil becomes, quite rightly, a figure of fun in the Christian tradition, and Catholics have a certain divinely won right to laugh in his face. We are of the Church of Peter, and the gates of hell (a defensive image from ancient siege warfare) shall not prevail against us.

Of course, this petition, like the whole of the Our Father, is corporate: "Deliver *us* from evil." Our prayer necessarily involves the whole of the Church in all her suffering, and in both heaven and earth, including the angels. Because there are devils, the Church has, from her inception, understood our deliverance from evil to involve the participation of both the saints and the angels. Revelation 12, in particular, associates the battle against the ancient dragon, who is called the devil and Satan, with the Blessed Virgin

Mary and with St. Michael the Archangel. Similarly, our prayers for those who are still being cleansed of the effects of sin and evil in their lives in purgatory are absolutely crucial because we are, as Paul points out, "members one of another" (Romans 12:5). The interconnectedness of the Communion of Saints is precisely one of the things the devil loathes the most because it is the opposite of pride, which is the sin that made the devil the devil.

Ultimately, our prayer to be delivered from evil is a prayer to be delivered from sin. The devil can throw all sorts of awful stuff at us, and some people have suffered horrible cruelties inspired by his malice. But if we do not break our communion with God by sinning against him, the critical aspect of the devil's mission has utterly failed. His goal is always to persuade us to imitate him in his rebellion. God can and does, when it is for our good and his glory, "deliver us from evil" in the sense of protecting us from hurts the devil may want to inflict on our circumstances. But sometimes, God will allow the devil to inflict grievous blows on this world and his saints, just as, in his own case, he allowed the lash, the crown of thorns, and the nails. But we can expect that when our hour comes, though "you will be hated by all for my name's sake," nonetheless "he who endures to the end will be saved" (Matthew 10:22).

So we pray:

> Deliver us, Lord, we pray, from every evil,
> graciously grant peace in our days
> that, by the help of your mercy,
> we may be always free from sin
> and safe from all distress,
> as we await the blessed hope
> and the coming of our Savior, Jesus Christ.[37]

PART TWO

THE HAIL MARY

Ave Maria, gratia plena, Dominus tecum.
Benedicta tu in mulieribus,
et benedictus fructus ventris tui, Iesus.
Sancta Maria, Mater Dei,
ora pro nobis peccatoribus,
nunc et in hora mortis nostrae. Amen.

———————————— ⌒ ————————————

Hail Mary, full of grace, the Lord is with thee.
Blessed art thou among women,
and blessed is the fruit of thy womb, Jesus.
Holy Mary, Mother of God,
pray for us sinners,
now and at the hour of our death. Amen.

Chapter 11

HAIL MARY

In the Old Testament, the standard protocol for angelic appearances is as follows:

1. The angel appears.
2. The human to whom he appears either
   a. does not realize he is an angel and so behaves as he would toward a fellow human being — that is, he makes the angel a nice meal and is hospitable, usually resulting in a blessing, or else, like the residents of Sodom, practices such forms of inhospitality as attempted homosexual gang rape, resulting in unpleasantness for the humans (Genesis 18-19)

or

   b. realizes from the get-go that he is speaking to an angel and promptly melts into a puddle of terror (e.g., Judges 6:22). This prompts the angel to issue the standard angelic greeting "Fear not!" followed by sundry efforts to get the human to pull himself back together, buck up, and pay attention since the angel (the very name means "messenger") is trying to deliver the Lord's message to the sniveling human who is trembling with terror at the encounter with this superhuman spiritual creature. After some preliminary "Woe is me . . . for I am a man of unclean lips, and I dwell in the midst of a people of unclean lips" (Isaiah 6:5) self-reproaches or a few "Wait! I am unworthy! Send somebody else!" (cf. Exodus 4:13) attempts to dodge the message or some "Could you give me a sign . . . or two . . . because I'm really unsure of myself" stabs at putting things off (cf. Judges 6:36-40), the human is sufficiently talked back down from his terror to be able to listen to the angel and begin stumbling through the mission he has been chosen for.

This is the background that lies behind the astonishing story of the archangel Gabriel's annunciation to the Blessed Virgin (Luke 1:26-38). In Luke, what we see is the archangel humbled before the human, while the human is, well, not afraid of him. She regards the angel with the eyes of one who seems to be used to staring into the sun. It's as though she knows the One who sent him so well that she's not dazzled by the presence of this lesser spiritual being. Gabriel isn't kidding when he says, "The Lord is with you!" (Luke 1:28). We do not get from her the normal breast-beating over her sinfulness. Indeed, it's as though she's not conscious of any sin on her part and feels nothing to be ashamed or abashed about. She is, to be sure, "troubled at the saying" (Luke 1:29) when the angel says, not "Fear not," but "Hail, full of grace" (Luke 1:28). That is, she is surprised and a bit fearful of the *message* but not of the messenger.

Like "Amen," "Hail" is a distinctly premodern word. We moderns use it as a joke when we pantomime our kowtows to puffed-up politicians we find ridiculous or when we cheer exaggeratedly for a sports star. We would regard somebody who used it in ordinary conversation as we would somebody who says "thou" or wears Shakespearean garb. That's because we live in a ruthlessly egalitarian age that has abandoned the snobbery and overt class-consciousness of antiquity at the cost of the courtesy and courtliness of antiquity.

Heaven preserves the courtesy without the snobbery. So the angel Gabriel, a creature vastly superior to humans in the natural order, bows to a young peasant Jewish girl and speaks with the utmost reverence and courtesy in language reserved for greeting a monarch or emperor. Normally, if you were a Roman, you said, "Hail *Caesar*!" But Gabriel bows himself before a teenager from some ditchwater town in a forgotten corner of Caesar's great empire and addresses *her* as royalty. This superhuman being, who has perhaps existed since before the Big Bang, who witnessed the breakup of the supercontinent Pangaea, the age of the dinosaurs, the formation of the Himalayas, and the long, slow anguish of the human race since the Fall, has come to this little house of sticks and stones in Nazareth to declare to this delicate thing of water, protein, and spirit that she is to give to Gabriel's God what Gabriel will never have: the flesh and blood of a man. Even more astonishingly, she consents — without three years of continual training like Peter, without getting blinded like Paul, without any of the long preliminary hesitations and backpedalings that characterize Moses, Gideon, Isaiah, or even her relative Zechariah. She hits the ground running — ready, willing, and able to say, "Let it be to me according to your word" (Luke 1:38).

The name of this girl — for girl she was and scarcely a woman — was Mary. It's a name with a long and honorable pedigree in the Jewish tradition, harking back to Moses' sister Miriam and to Naomi, the mother-in-law of Ruth, an ancestor of David (Exodus 15:20; Ruth 1:20). Curiously, it means "bitter," which is not the sort of thing upscale American parents are looking for as they peruse the baby books for power names like "Madison" and "Tiffany" and dream of a daughter with a five-hundred-dollar suit, a cell phone glued to her ear, high cheekbones, severe glasses, a tough corporate handshake, and the sexual prowess to melt the heart of a competitor just enough so that he won't see the hostile takeover till the barracuda's jaws snap shut.

These are, after all, the things we celebrate these days in all the commanding heights of culture, from New York to Washington, DC, to Los Angeles. They are a million miles from the weakness and vulnerability of a woman whose life was destined, by divine prophecy, to be bitter indeed. Mary's self-surrendering virginity says, "It's about love, not power." To the power addict who can only conceive of a world neatly divided between the cunning and the stupid, Mary's way is the way of death. So, for instance, Simone de Beauvoir recoils from such surrender when she writes of Mary:

> For the first time in history the mother kneels before her son; she freely accepts her inferiority. This is the supreme masculine victory, consummated in the cult of the Virgin — it is the rehabilitation of woman through the accomplishment of her defeat.[38]

For surrender is death, according to the world. So the world produces men and women who distill the worship of power down to truly bitter dregs, to gain the whole world while losing their own souls. But Mary's surrender to God leads to the mystery of total dependence on God — and the paradox of happiness through the bitter cross. The Son before whom she kneels is not some selfish boor of this fallen world but the Second Adam, who undergoes a defeat far more profound than her own self-surrender so that he may exalt her to a glory above all other creatures. In him and him alone, power and love are reconciled, and we find, not servility crushed by domination, but humility crowned with glory.

That's why Gabriel bows to her. For, as St. Padre Pio said, angels envy us in this alone; they cannot suffer with Christ as we can.[39] Mary is hailed because the strange favor of God is with her, bestowing on her the bitterness of the Mother of Sorrows, whose heart will be pierced by the same lance that pierced the heart of her Son (Luke 2:35; John 19:34) — and who will receive a glory second only to his when she sees him risen and, in due time, she herself shares in his risen life in the Assumption, when she takes her place above even Gabriel.

That's why Tradition teaches us, in the Hail Mary, to first look at her with the eyes of the angels and see the holy envy she ignites in them. For where she is, we too will one day be, if we continue in faith in her Son as she did to the very end of ends.

Chapter 12

FULL OF GRACE

At the time Gabriel appeared to Mary, an emperor ruled the known world. His name was Augustus Caesar. Caesar, while originally a proper name, had already begun to morph into a title (a title that would be preserved in such words as Czar and Kaiser). In short, Augustus and his successors were spoken of by his title, not his name.

Mary, too, is addressed by a title when Gabriel appears to her saying, "*Kaire, Kecharitomene!*" (Luke 1:28). It's a title that is too full of meaning to render accurately in English. "Hail, Full-of-Grace!" is part of it. "Hail! Highly Favored One" is another part of it. "Hail! Full-of-Divine-Life!" touches on it as well.

The Western tradition, especially in the Rosary, has settled on "*Gratia Plena,*" or "Full-of-Grace," as the preferred rendering. In this title, the Catholic tradition has always seen the biblical reflection of the Church's ancient apostolic faith in the sinlessness of Mary.

Note that I say "reflection" and not "basis." That's because the Church is not "based on the Bible" but is rather based on the Word made flesh. The Bible does not come first and then the Church gets built on top of it, "deriving" various doctrines from tenuous and ambiguous sentence fragments here and there as though some medieval pope said to his secretary one day, "Oh look! Here's a passage where Gabriel calls Mary 'full of grace'! How about we say, on the basis of this passing reference, that . . . ummmmm . . . oh, I don't know . . . how about 'Mary is immaculately conceived and preserved from all sin, both original and actual'? Think people will buy that whopper? It's just wild enough that they may go for it!"

Rather, the belief in Mary's sinlessness is already implicit in the faith of the apostles, and the biblical passage is the *reflection* of the apostolic teaching that goes out to all the Churches with the preaching of the apostles. That's why, from east to west, across a dozen different cultures, tongues, and rites of the ancient Church, the overwhelming consensus of the Fathers of the Church is that Mary is "most pure,"[40] "formed without any stain,"[41] "all-Holy,"[42] "undefiled,"[43] "spotless,"[44] "immaculate of the immaculate,"[45] "inviolate and free from every stain of sin,"[46] and created in a condition more sublime and glorious than all other natures.[47]

In short, for the Fathers, as for the Catholic Church, Mary is as St. Ephraem describes her:

> Most holy Lady, Mother of God, alone most pure in soul and body, alone exceeding all perfection of purity . . . alone made in thy entirety the home of all the graces of the Most Holy Spirit, and hence exceeding beyond all compare even the angelic virtues in purity and sanctity of soul and body . . . my Lady most holy, all-pure, all-immaculate, all-stainless, all-undefiled, all-incorrupt, all-inviolate spotless robe of Him Who clothes Himself with light as with a garment . . . flower unfading, purple woven by God, alone most immaculate.[48]

This is not because everybody in the early Church simultaneously began building the same gigantic mountain of Marian sinlessness on the same textual molehill in Luke 1. It is, instead, because the apostles, wherever they founded their Churches, taught that Mary was sinless and that their disciples should therefore read Gabriel's words through that interpretive lens of apostolic Tradition.

The implication of the title is astounding and beautiful, but what stands out in comparison to the pagan Roman greeting is how humble it is. Mary is who she is, not because she schemed her way to the top or rubbed out her competitors, but because she is the least and is entirely sustained by God's grace. She is not full of grace because she has exalted herself. Rather, she is exalted because she is full of grace. As she herself said, "He has put down the mighty from their thrones, and exalted those of low degree" (Luke 1:52).

In all this, of course, we find the reflection of God's even greater humility. For as Chesterton notes in his beautiful poem "Gloria in Profundis," God is second to none in his eagerness to humble himself:

There has fallen on earth for a token
A god too great for the sky.
He has burst out of all things and broken
The bounds of eternity:
Into time and the terminal land
He has strayed like a thief or a lover,
For the wine of the world brims over,
Its splendour is split on the sand.

Who is proud when the heavens are humble,
Who mounts if the mountains fall,
If the fixed stars topple and tumble
And a deluge of love drowns all-
Who rears up his head for a crown,
Who holds up his will for a warrant,
Who strives with the starry torrent,
When all that is good goes down?

For in dread of such falling and failing
The fallen angels fell
Inverted in insolence, scaling
The hanging mountain of hell:
But unmeasured of plummet and rod
Too deep for their sight to scan,
Outrushing the fall of man
Is the height of the fall of God.

Glory to God in the Lowest
The spout of the stars in spate-
Where thunderbolt thinks to be slowest
And the lightning fears to be late:

As men dive for sunken gem
Pursuing, we hunt and hound it,
The fallen star has found it
In the cavern of Bethlehem.[49]

The fullness of grace that brimmed over in her filled not merely her heart but also her womb, as the grace of the God who is more humble than she was made flesh and dwelt among us. For the grace that filled Mary was not a theological abstraction or a sentiment. It was a baby.

Chapter 13

THE LORD IS WITH THEE

One of the things that mark the writers of the New Testament is their appreciation for the fact that, since Scripture is primarily the work of the Holy Spirit and not merely of human authors, it therefore conveys more meaning than merely human words. So the New Testament writers read Old Testament Scripture looking for meanings beyond the literal sense of the words. They did this, not because they were crazy Dark Age nuts who decided to treat Jewish holy books as a Rorschach blot upon which to project their own *ex post facto* Christian fantasies, but because the Risen Christ met them on the Road to Emmaus and said:

> "These are my words which I spoke to you, while I was still with you, that everything written about me in the law of Moses and the prophets and the psalms must be fulfilled." Then he opened their minds to understand the scriptures, and said to them, "Thus it is written, that the Christ should suffer and on the third day rise from the dead, and that repentance and forgiveness of sins should be preached in his name to all nations, beginning from Jerusalem." (Luke 24:44-47)

In short, it is from Jesus that the Church gets the idea that everything revealed in the New Testament was hidden in the Old. This way of reading Scripture is, for instance, what enables Jesus to see that the manna in the wilderness (Exodus 16) is a divine foreshadow of himself, the true Bread of Life (John 6). It is why Paul says that the passage of Israel through the Red Sea (Exodus 14) is a divine foreshadow of Baptism (1 Corinthians 10:1-6). It is how John sees in the unbroken bones of the Passover lamb (Exodus

12:46) a divine foreshadow of the unbroken bones of the Lamb of God, who takes away the sin of the world (John 19:33-35).

The Church sees these other senses of Scripture not only in looking for Christ in the Old Testament but in seeing other aspects of the Christian revelation as well. So, for instance, in Romans 8:36, Paul looks at Psalm 44, which was written as a lament for the sufferings of Israel in a time of national disaster, and sees in the innocent suffering of the psalmist a foreshadowing of the innocent sufferings of persecuted Christians. Likewise, Peter takes the description of Israel as a "kingdom of priests and a holy nation" (Exodus 19:6) and applies it to the Church (1 Peter 2:9), since he regards the Church as the New Israel.

Matthew is doing the same thing when he cites Isaiah's famous Emmanuel prophecy in his infancy narrative: "All this took place to fulfill what the Lord had spoken by the prophet, 'Behold, a virgin shall conceive and bear a son, and his name shall be called Emmanuel' (which means, God with us)" (Matthew 1:22-23).

This sign, like most of the signs of the Old Testament, has an immediate fulfillment in the Old Testament setting. However, that does not mean the sign has been drained of meaning by its immediate fulfillment and can now be disposed of. Rather, as is the way with God, we discover that Old Testament signs go on becoming even more meaningful with the passage of time.

To illustrate, consider Moses' promise to Israel:

> "The LORD your God will raise up for you a prophet like me from among you, from your brethren — him you shall heed — just as you desired of the LORD your God at Horeb on the day of the assembly, when you said, 'Let me not hear again the voice of the LORD my God, or see this great fire any more, lest I die.' And the LORD said to me, 'They have rightly said all that they have spoken. I will raise up for them a prophet like you from among their brethren; and I will put my words in his mouth, and he shall speak to them all that I

command him. And whoever will not give heed to my words which he shall speak in my name, I myself will require it of him.' " (Deuteronomy 18:15-19)

In fact, of course, there are multiple Old Testament fulfillments of this promise. Elijah, Elisha, Isaiah, Jeremiah, Ezekiel, Daniel, Hosea, and the rest of the noble company of Old Testament prophets are all fulfillments of Moses' promise to Israel that a prophet like him would arise. But the fascinating thing is that Jews at the time of the New Testament did not look at the prophets and say, "So *that's* over with. Prophecy fulfilled. Expect nothing further." Instead, they saw these Old Testament prophets as a divine foreshadow of some great and ultimate prophet who was yet to come. That's why the delegation from Jerusalem asked John the Baptist, "Are you *the* prophet?" (John 1:21, emphasis added). Jews at the time of Christ were still expecting the One whom all the prophets of the Old Testament foreshadowed.

Exactly the same thing obtains with the One whom the prophets refer to variously as the Son of David, the Servant of the Lord, the Branch, the Star Out of Jacob, the Anointed One, and the Messiah. There are, in fact, lots of sons of David, some good, some not so good. When one of the "sons of David" — namely, King Ahaz — is in deep trouble five hundred years after David, the prophet Isaiah goes to him, reminds him that God is still with the house of David, and tells him to ask for any sign in proof of that fact. Ahaz refuses, so Isaiah returns to him, chews him out for his faithlessness, and then declares: "Therefore the Lord himself will give you a sign. Behold, a young woman shall conceive and bear a son, and shall call his name Immanuel" (Isaiah 7:14).

The immediate fulfillment of this promise takes place shortly thereafter with the birth of Ahaz' son, Hezekiah, to the "*almah*" or "young woman" Isaiah speaks of (namely, Ahaz' wife).[50] But that doesn't exhaust the meaning of the prophecy for Matthew, because for the evangelist, *Hezekiah himself becomes a sign* pointing forward to the *ultimate* Son of David, who is born, not merely of a young woman, but of a virgin. Some debunkers will tell you that Matthew believes that Jesus was born of a virgin because of a textual error, since the pre-Christian Jewish translators of the Septuagint rendered the Hebrew *almah* (young woman) as the Greek *parthenos* (virgin) and that it is this translation that Matthew cites in his Gospel. The problem with this theory is that Matthew does not get his information about the birth of Jesus from Isaiah. He gets it from the only possible source: the Blessed Virgin Mary. It is only after hearing it from her that he reads Isaiah in its Greek form and realizes the connection of the Emmanuel prophecy to Jesus.

In this, the parallel with the apostles' behavior at the mouth of the empty tomb is striking. Just as they "did not know the scripture, that he must rise from the dead" (John 20:9), even when standing at the mouth of the empty tomb and, indeed, even when the Risen Christ himself is explaining Scripture to them personally on the Emmaus road (cf. John 20:9; Luke 24:15-16), likewise it is only *after* the Church has received the story of the Virgin Birth from the Blessed Virgin herself and has been enlightened by the Holy Spirit that they finally smack themselves on the forehead, read the Old Testament, and say, "It's been staring us in the face the whole time." As Paul says, the mystery is veiled until the Holy Spirit takes away the veil (2 Corinthians 3:14-15).

So Matthew does not *derive* his faith in the Virgin Birth from Isaiah 7:14. Rather, he sees the Virgin Birth prophetically *reflected* there, both in the birth of Hezekiah the Son of David and in the curiously providential way that the Greek translation of the Old Testament speaks of the Son of David as the son of a Virgin. His purpose in quoting the passage is to remind the reader that Jesus is not a hiccup or an aberration in the history of Israel but the whole point of the story. Everything has been leading up to him, the ultimate Son of David, who now sits upon the throne of David, from everlasting to everlasting, as Nathan promised David.

It is, therefore, no accident that the words of the angel to Mary are "The Lord is with you" and that the name given the Messianic Son of David in Isaiah 7:14 is "Immanuel" — "God with us." Mary is a kind of icon of the whole Church. As God was with her by being present in her womb, so he is with us on the altar, when we receive him into our body and soul in the Eucharist.

Chapter 14

BLESSED ART THOU AMONG WOMEN

One common complaint among many Protestant evangelicals, my old stomping ground, is that Catholics honor Mary "too much." It's a highly specialized complaint, much like the common evangelical complaint about Catholic "graven images" that completely overlooks the evangelical's own bowling trophies. After all — and I speak from experience here as someone in recovery from "Mariaphobic Response Syndrome" — evangelicals have no problem honoring Paul. They write hundreds of books about him, talk about his holiness and genius in thousands of sermons, and generally hold him up as a shining model of Christian greatness — as they should. They rightly observe that, if not for Paul, the Gospel would never have reached the Gentile world.

But I began to realize there was often an odd choking sensation among us evangelicals when Catholics noted with equal truth that without Mary, the Gospel would have never reached the planet. The conversation chilled under an icy cloud of fear and a sense of menace, as though we were worried that the person saying this was just about to break out in a frenzy of goddess worship. Strange caveats and backpedalings ensued. We suddenly felt compelled to insist that Mary's yes to God meant nothing unique *at all* about her role in salvation history, and to press the claim that she certainly is deserving of no special mentions. We said, in a curiously rapid way, that God would just as easily have chosen somebody else, as though we had full access to the inner counsels of the divine mind as he surveys an infinitude of alternate universes.

It began to bug me that we reserved this kind of talk for Mary, while nobody in the evangelical world ever felt the need to talk this way about Paul. When it came to him, we remained in *this* universe, looking at *what God actually did* rather than flying off to a billion other hypothetical universes to pontificate about what God surely would have done.

Similarly, it began to bother me that when Mary herself declares in Luke 1:48, "For behold, henceforth all generations will call me blessed," we evangelicals typically felt an ungovernable compulsion to declare that, since Scripture likewise speaks of Jael as blessed among women (Judges 5:24), we can safely say that Mary is no big deal. Yet, strangely, we felt no similar compulsion to diminish Jesus when Isaiah calls Cyrus the Lord's "anointed" (i.e., "Messiah"; Isaiah 45:1). In Jesus' case, we recognized that Cyrus was a divine foreshadow of Jesus the liberator, just as the manna, the parting of the Red Sea, and Hezekiah were likewise types and shadows of the Gospel. It was only in the case of the Blessed Virgin that we refused to see Jael as a prophetic foreshadow and instead turned her into a rival of the Mother of the Anointed One, who is most blessed among women.

Eventually, I could see no sense to this irrational prejudice against Mary. At the end of the day, Jesus Christ is God Incarnate and Cyrus is not, just as Mary is the Mother of God Incarnate and Jael is not. Mary freely said yes to giving God the Son the flesh and blood by which he would achieve the redemption of the world on the cross. In *this* universe, and not some hypothetical one, she assented, not just to the conception of Christ, but also to the days to come, day by day, for more than thirty years, until the moment she had to stand there, absolutely helpless, and watch him die the most shameful and unjust death any mother has ever had to endure, under a cruel and despotic regime in some third-world hellhole. In short, just as we would surely honor not just a fallen soldier but also his grieving parents at the soldier's funeral, so the Catholic Church has always very sensibly paid honor to the Mother of our Captain, who threw himself on the grenade of sin, hell, and death to save his troops, and who died in combat against the forces of hell. Not to do so is churlish.

That's why I finally realized that the real question is not "Don't Catholics honor Mary too much?" but rather "Where exactly did we evangelicals honor her 'just enough'?" And it's why I eventually concluded that the reality is that Catholics honor her as she should be honored, while one would have to search a very long time in evangelical circles to find any honor paid to her at all — and with such an honor being made quite grudgingly and timidly, filled with continual hesitations and a continual odor of deep fear of her.

That's a fact noted even by honest evangelical scholars like Timothy George.[51] Apart from "Round yon Virgin Mother and Child" at Christmas (a verse written by a Catholic,[52] by the by), veneration and honor of the Blessed Virgin is almost nonexistent in evangelical circles. So I came to realize that the complaint by evangelicals that Catholics honor Mary "too much" is like the tee-totaler telling the normal man who likes a glass of wine at dinner that every sip is "drinking to excess."

As we move away from these controversies and look closer to home, we find another dynamic at work. Even within the Catholic communion, the Church is often complained of as "dominated by men." To converts from an evangelical background filled with jitters about Mary, this is hilarious. For what hits us converts in the face is not the masculinity but the femininity of the Church. In other words, so much of the Church's prayer, life, and practice is Marian, contemplative, receptive, inward, body-centered, and Eucharistic, while so much of Protestant (and especially American evangelical) Christianity is Pauline, aggressive, word-centered, mission-oriented, and focused on getting a job done. Both the masculine and feminine approaches to the faith are good and biblical, but it should be noted that the feminine way is particularly rooted in the Church's reverence for Mary, who is "blessed among women."

Mary is, in the end, called "blessed" not merely because of her suffering, nor merely because she did or said this or that. Indeed, Scripture does not contain an Acts of Mary because it is precisely her part, in the economy of salvation, not so much to do as to *be.* Her characteristic posture is contemplative: she "kept all these things in her heart" (Luke 2:51). Her characteristic gesture is to refer us to her Son: "Do whatever he tells you" (John 2:5). Her sole literary legacy is a hymn of praise that magnifies God, not herself (Luke 1:46-55). That does not make her a wallflower or a cipher. It makes her the most fully saved human being who ever lived — saved from sin completely, not by the desperate rescue from the pit that the rest of us have fallen into, but by being kept from the pit in the first place by the grace of her Son. This, in turn, makes her the freest creature God ever made, not an automaton. For "where the Spirit of the Lord is, there is freedom" (2 Corinthians 3:17).

This curiously quiet and hidden place in the Kingdom of God, so far from the very public and dramatic trials and tribulations of the apostles, with their Indiana Jones adventures and globetrotting ways, is why Mary's enormous powers — what John Paul II called "other and greater powers"[53] than those of the apostles — is often overlooked. Her power in the life of the Church is like air pressure or sunlight or gravity. You don't think about it. It's always there, in the background, the power of the entire prayer life of the Church, quietly interceding for the noisier and more visible members, calm and relentless as a river, seemingly weak, but able in the long run to grind the Himalayas down to dust. And she does it all in the peace of Christ, whom she loved from her very heart from the first moment of her creation and will be praising and loving when the last atoms of this passing world are gone. Blessed, truly, is she among women.

Chapter 15

AND BLESSED IS THE FRUIT OF THY WOMB, JESUS

Those of us struggling with or in recovery from Mariaphobic Response Syndrome have certain passages and prayers that fill us with a nameless dread. The title of this chapter is one of them. Here, more than anywhere, there's a certain gynecological something that sends people from my evangelical background hurrying to the Bible to look for ways to *diminish* Mary by any means necessary. The fear, though we seldom get around to articulating it, is a sort of mishmash of fretfulness about idolatry, the power of the feminine, and just the frightened apprehension that all this "blessing Mary" stuff is bound to lead to goddess worship. As we've already seen, we tend to dwell on selected Bible verses to emphasize that Mary isn't special. Indeed, so zealous was the tendency of some Christians from my old evangelical neighborhood to diminish Mary that we even liked to bang away at things Scripture does *not* say about Mary.

Take for starters these little samples from various anti-Catholic websites laboring to purge Christianity of Mary:

- "Please note that Mary is NOT the 'Mother of God,' as God was around long before Mary was born. Mary is the mother of Jesus (Acts 1:14), she is never called the 'Mother of God.' Jesus never called Mary 'mother,' but 'woman.' "[54]
- "The divine nature of Jesus existed from before eternity, and this cannot be said of Mary. Jesus never called her 'mother.' He called her 'woman.' "[55]
- "Remember, Jesus never called Mary Mother."[56]

By this strange method of reading Scripture, such anti-Marian logic also "proves" that Jesus never sneezed, never laughed, and never blinked, since these actions, too, are not recorded in Scripture. But this appears to be a small price to pay to shove the threatening Virgin into the closet and away from polite company.

Indeed, the deeper you go into the psyche of the determined anti-Marian, the stranger things get. As we see above, one of the oddest tendencies of those bound and determined to get rid of Mary is the peculiar insistence that Love Incarnate somehow had a relationship with his mother that was more alienated and cold than the one Joan Crawford's daughter had with her "Mommie Dearest."

This weird portrayal of the relationship between Jesus and Mary, with Jesus as the icy and aloof son who won't call his mother "Mother," can result in the complete dehumanization of the Virgin. The sheer gynecological disgust of the critic grows . . .

> Mary did what women do. What animals do. There is only one command that mankind at large obeys, and that is to reproduce. It requires no brains, no nobility, no courage, no faith, no virtue.[57]

. . . and grows . . .

> Mary was just an incubator. All she supplied was a virgin womb. God was both Father AND Mother of Jesus, Who was the Word, NOT Mary's ovum made flesh.[58]

. . . and grows . . .

> Jesus **COULD NOT** in any way have proceeded from the genetics of the fallen, degenerated human race. The undeniable truth is that the chromosomes of the child Jesus did not come from Joseph, but they also did not come from Mary. . . . Mary's womb was chosen by the Creator to give form to His Human Image. The initial cell of that Human

Image, with its 46 chromosomes, originated from the Throne of *"the Majesty on High"* (Hebrews 1:3). Mary's womb was the special "incubator" used by the Eternal One to initiate and form the *"Word of God"* which was *"made flesh."* The blood from Mary's womb was used by God to protect and feed the embryo, which then became a fetus, which then became the holy child that was born. However, the blood that began flowing through the veins of that Special Human Being had absolutely nothing to do with the blood of the womb from where He was formed throughout the gestational period. For many centuries, the spirit of the deceiver has presented Mary as divine, blasphemously converting her into the "Mother of God."[59]

Finally, in the effort to save Jesus from contact with Mary, he is ultimately "saved" from membership in the human race and becomes instead the sole member of a brand new species, born of an egg created *ex nihilo* and implanted by divine *in vitro* fertilization into an incubator unit he coldly refuses to call "Mother." Of course, that means Jesus can't save us from the death that Adam brought into the world since he is no longer a member of the human race capable of undoing what Adam did. But that is a small price to pay for some Christians if only the terrifying specter of Mary can be dispelled.

Now, most evangelicals don't go to quite these lengths to exorcise Mary from the Christian faith, but most of them do feel keenly the desire to, at any rate, keep Mary at arm's length. I matured as a young Christian in an environment that constantly taught me to assume that Jesus had an awkward and cold relationship with his mother; a relationship that looks rather like the awkward and cold relationship most evangelicals have with her.

The biblical arguments supporting our picture of things were varied and not infrequently flatly contradictory, but they tended to agree that Mary was, at best, basically a crummy disciple and

somebody we would be well advised not to imitate, let alone vener-
ate. So, for instance, back in my evangelical days, we typically took it
for granted that Jesus "rebuked" his mother at the Wedding at Cana
(John 2:1-11) for her too-worldly enthusiasm for him as Messiah:

> Catholicism says that our Lord's mother was immaculate,
> but if this were true she could not have incurred our Lord's
> rebuke. . . . Catholicism teaches that Mary's intercession is
> recognized by Christ. But this is the only instance on record
> of such intercession, and though it was addressed to Christ
> while in the flesh and was concerning a purely temporal mat-
> ter, it was promptly rebuked. . . . Our Lord's answer indi-
> cates that Mary's request had in it more than a desire for the
> gift of wine. What she principally wanted was to have Jesus
> manifest himself as Messiah.[60]

Here, the charge is that Mary was so bursting with a sort of
crass worldly faith in Jesus that she wanted to boss him around
and impress the neighbors with "My Son the Messiah." On this
accounting, Jesus had to tell her to pipe down with her fleshly
demands for miraculous stunts and distance himself from her,
something he was pretty much always trying to do in the evangelical picture of their relationship.

However, in the next breath, we would also assert that Mary
hardly had *any* faith in Jesus and that Jesus also rebuked her for
that. We usually did that by recourse to this famous scene from
the Gospels:

> Then he went home; and the crowd came together again, so
> that they could not even eat. And when his family heard it,
> they went out to seize him, for people were saying, "He is
> beside himself." And the scribes who came down from Jeru-
> salem said, "He is possessed by Beelzebul, and by the prince
> of demons he casts out the demons." And he called them to
> him, and said to them in parables, "How can Satan cast out

Satan? If a kingdom is divided against itself, that kingdom cannot stand. And if a house is divided against itself, that house will not be able to stand. And if Satan has risen up against himself and is divided, he cannot stand, but is coming to an end. But no one can enter a strong man's house and plunder his goods, unless he first binds the strong man; then indeed he may plunder his house.

"Truly, I say to you, all sins will be forgiven the sons of men, and whatever blasphemies they utter; but whoever blasphemes against the Holy Spirit never has forgiveness, but is guilty of an eternal sin" — for they had said, "He has an unclean spirit."

And his mother and his brethren came; and standing outside they sent to him and called him. And a crowd was sitting about him; and they said to him, "Your mother and your brethren are outside, asking for you." And he replied, "Who are my mother and my brethren?" And looking around on those who sat about him, he said, "Here are my mother and my brethren! Whoever does the will of God is my brother, and sister, and mother." (Mark 3:19-35)

Relying on *this* scene, I was frequently informed that Mary had virtually no faith in Jesus. As one typical "Bible teacher" puts it:

Mary was not VERY spiritual. She was a believer in God. She did accept God's will for her life, to be the mother of Jesus on His human side. But she was not the intensely holy and very spiritual person we are often led to believe. For example, here in Mark 3:21 we see her belief about Jesus that led her to take her other sons to go "take charge of Him" and bring Him home. . . .

"He is out of His mind." Mary believed Jesus to be a bit crazy, and that explained his traveling around the countryside preaching, and taking on disciples, etc. Is this a spiritual attitude toward Jesus? I think it rather reveals a certain lack of faith, during these early stages of Jesus' ministry.[61]

So "during these early stages of Jesus' ministry," Mary believed in Jesus as the Messiah of God way too much and Jesus "rebuked" her for that, according to the evangelical reading of the miracle at Cana, and yet she also rejected Jesus as the Messiah and joined in the crowd and the Pharisees' jeering at him as a demon-possessed lunatic (Mark 3:21, 30). So, again, Jesus "rebuked" this (allegedly) well-nigh faithless woman and publicly shamed her by counting any random disciple as more important than she was. The one constant in both of these evangelical tellings of the Gospel was that Jesus wanted as little to do with Mary as possible and took almost any occasion as a chance to dis her.

This account of things began to look pretty dodgy to me. How could Mary have a too-zealous faith in Jesus as Messiah while also thinking him possessed by an unclean spirit? I recalled Chesterton's warning: "If you hear a thing being accused of being too tall and too short, too red and too green, too bad in one way and too bad also in the opposite way, then you may be sure that it is very good."[62] I again began to realize that "Mary as worldly Jewish stage mother pushing her complaining and reluctant son onto the stage of history" and "Mary joining in the denunciation of Jesus as a demon-possessed lunatic" were precisely the sort of mutually contradictory charges that, in fact, said much more about evangelical jitters about (and alienation from) Mary than they said about the scriptural portrayal of the Blessed Virgin.

This sensation only increased when I noticed that the accounts in John, Mark, and Luke really didn't support the strange hostility to Mary that we Mariaphobes brought to the text. Mary, for example, is not "rebuked" by Jesus at the Wedding at Cana. Rather, she is *challenged* by him. He knows what she wants when she says, "They have no wine." She knows that he knows what she wants: for him to reveal himself to Israel in the great sign of Messianic bounty brimming with wine (Isaiah 25:6-8), which John will later call the "marriage feast of the Lamb" and which Jesus himself repeatedly calls a wedding feast (cf. Revelation 19:6-9; Matthew 22:1-4). So far from rebuking her, *Jesus does as she asks* after he challenges her to display just the importunate prayer of trust he desires of his disciples (Luke 18:1-8). She does not back down, and Jesus does not expect her to do so. Instead, she tells the servants, as she still tells us, "Do whatever he tells you" (John 2:5). That pretty much summarizes the whole of her message to us ever since.

Similarly, despite the evangelical determination to see Mary somehow joining in the mob that denounced Jesus as "having an unclean spirit," I, in fact, discovered that it is not Mary but "people" who were saying this (Mark 3:21). Nothing in the text substantiates the claim that Mary doubted him, much less called him crazy or demon possessed. What the text *does* suggest is that Mary was concerned for his safety and went along with the family to protect him, just as Paul's disciples were likewise concerned that a mob would lay violent hands on him (Acts 19:30-31). That's hardly a sin. Nor did Jesus' response to the mention of his mother show that he denied her honor. How could he, since it was his own Spirit who had commanded Israel via the Law of Moses to "Honor your father and mother" (Exodus 20:12)? Indeed, this passage in Mark 3, which so many of us evangelicals took as yet another swipe at Mary, turned out to mean that if you have faith, you are a lot like Mary.

How did I know that? Paradoxically, because of the king of all allegedly anti-Marian passages: "As he said this, a woman in the crowd raised her voice and said to him, 'Blessed is the womb that bore you, and the breasts that you sucked!' But he said, 'Blessed rather are those who hear the word of God and keep it!' " (Luke 11:27-28).

Surely here, I had been taught, we have a direct rebuke to the notion that we should honor Jesus' mother — with that telling word "rather" to emphasize the point. So it would seem. Yet, as I studied Luke's Gospel, I was confronted with the fact that if this passage meant what my evangelical background insisted it must mean, then what were we to make of Mary's cousin Elizabeth when she cries out, under the inspiration of the Spirit, "Blessed are you among women, and blessed is the fruit of your womb!" (Luke 1:42)? She said exactly what the woman in the crowd had said! Indeed, even Mary herself, speaking under the inspiration of the Holy Spirit, says, "Henceforth all generations will call me *blessed*" (Luke 1:48, emphasis added), not "Henceforth all generations will get chewed out by Jesus for calling me blessed." Even God — whose angel called her *Kecharitomene*, "Full-of-Grace," "Highly Favored One" — had no problem heaping praise on Mary.

Knowing that God cannot contradict himself therefore prompted me to question my Mariaphobic assumptions still more deeply. Is Jesus, the fruit of her womb, saying that the fruit of her womb is *not* blessed? That can't be right. Was Jesus saying that Mary is not blessed? God, Gabriel, and Elizabeth certainly thought she was. So, for that matter, did Luke since he is, after all, the one who carefully recorded Gabriel's, Elizabeth's, and Mary's words for future generations to pray and ponder. So what gives?

Jesus' words to the woman in the crowd only constitute a rebuke of Marian devotion if Mary had not heard the word of God and kept it. But, in fact, Luke has taken great pains, more than any other Gospel writer, to carefully detail that Mary did most emphatically hear the word of God and keep it. He knows what Mary's response to the word of God was: "Let it be to me according to your word!" (Luke 1:38). Luke has already specifically told us that Mary "*kept* all these things in her heart" (Luke 2:51, emphasis added). In other words, Luke knows that Mary is the exemplar of the disciple who hears the word of God and keeps it. His point in recording Jesus' remark in chapter 11 of his Gospel is the same as his point in recording chapters 1 and 2: he wants us to understand that Mary was not blessed because she gave birth; she gave birth because she was blessed — blessed with the gift of faith to obey God with her yes. In short, Luke is making the same point Jesus did when he said:

"A sound tree cannot bear evil fruit, nor can a bad tree bear good fruit. Every tree that does not bear good fruit is cut down and thrown into the fire. Thus you will know them by their fruits." (Matthew 7:18-20)

The fruit that Mary's faith bore was Jesus Christ himself! Think about that. Paul, in a fit of pique at the thickheaded Galatians, once exhorted the Galatians to get with the program and start acting like disciples saved by faith in Christ and not by their own strength and power. He wrote, "My little children, with whom I am again in travail *until Christ be formed in you!*" (Galatians 4:19, emphasis added). That's an image from pregnancy. Paul is demanding that the disciples bring the fetal Christ to birth in their lives and nurture him to maturity in their souls.

Now, who is our role model for this image of Christ being formed in us by persistent faith and obedience to the word of God? There is only one person in history who could possibly be the template for such an image. In Mary, the Word became, not a metaphor, or an idea, or a spiritual concept, but *flesh*. It is precisely due to God's grace working in her and giving her enormous faith and obedience to Jesus' Father that Mary could do this. Paul's image and Jesus' exhortation to the woman in the crowd in Luke 11 both recall what Jesus said in Mark 3: that all who do his Father's will are his mother. We, therefore, do well to praise her and the fruit of her womb, that we might imitate her and likewise enflesh the word of God in what we do, say, and think.

It is, therefore, for us to bear good fruit as Mary did by bringing into the world another saint conformed to Christ's image, blessed to share in the fruit of her womb, Jesus, and through Baptism to enter into the mystery of her spiritual maternity that Jesus inaugurated when he made her our Mother too with the words: "Behold, your mother" (John 19:27). That saint is you, and Mary is your Mother and model of discipleship.

Chapter 16

HOLY MARY, MOTHER OF GOD

In the Gospel of Luke, the angel Gabriel tells Mary, "The Holy Spirit will come upon you, and the power of the Most High will overshadow you; therefore the child to be born will be called holy, the Son of God" (Luke 1:35).

Some critics of Marian devotion look at this and say, "Notice that it is Jesus, not Mary, whom the angel calls 'holy.' But Catholics, with their misplaced emphasis, instead pray 'Holy Mary, Mother of God.' In their ignorance of Scripture, they do not realize that God alone is holy!"

The problem with this sort of statement is that it nicely illustrates Josh Billings' old saying, "The trouble with people is not that they don't know, but that they know so much that ain't so." The notion that God alone is holy is one of those things that people know that ain't so.

To be sure, both Catholic and biblical language sometimes seem to suggest that God alone is holy. For instance, in the *Gloria* we are taught to pray: "For you alone are the Holy One, you alone are the Lord, you alone are the Most High, Jesus Christ, with the Holy Spirit, in the glory of God the Father. Amen."[63] But this does not mean the same thing as "You alone are holy." It means "You alone are God, the Holy One." How do we know? Because Scripture is quite emphatic that there are lots of things and people that are "holy to the Lord." So, for instance, Israel is commanded to keep the Sabbath holy (Exodus 20:8). They themselves are called "holy to the LORD" in Deuteronomy 7:6, and the sundry paraphernalia of their worship, the temple vessels, altars, offerings, and priestly garments, for instance, are likewise called holy. Nor does this cease in the New Testament, for Peter succinctly commands us, "As obedient children, do not be conformed to the passions of your former ignorance, but as he who called you is holy, be holy yourselves in all your conduct; since it is written, 'You shall be holy, for I am holy' " (1 Peter 1:14-16).

That's because to be holy does not mean "to be God" but "to be set apart." It is, like many sacred things, related to an ordinary human tendency and then exalted by grace. In this case, it is the tendency to set things apart that are precious to us. We don't use a wedding dress to wrap a fish in, or toss our late father's watch in the trash even though it's broken, or treat the sacred space and time of a funeral as an occasion to loudly shoot the breeze about baseball in the back pew. We hallow all sorts of things, places, people, dates, and times. God does it too when he sets apart certain people, places, times, and things to reveal himself to us.

It is telling that the command to be holy comes from a book (Leviticus 11:44) that is partly concerned with moral behavior but primarily concerned with prescriptions for cultic rites and prohibitions against various forms of ritual uncleanness. Here again, we see in Israel's conflation of moral precepts and ritual rules that very common phenomenon in antiquity to blur the lines or, more precisely, not to have yet created the lines between things that would subsequently get teased apart. So just as pagan thinkers like the Magi had not yet made clear category distinctions between what we will later call "magic," "science," "religion," "astronomy," and "astrology," so the book of Leviticus likewise had no sharp distinctions between what we now call "ritual impurity" and what we now call "moral impurity." The ancient Israelite saw no sharp distinction between eating pork and, say, blaspheming God or robbing an old man. All were regarded as acts that "defile." But what "defile" meant had not yet been ironed out in the earliest parts of the Old Testament.*

---

* By the way, before we get too impressed with ourselves about progressing past those silly Old Testament dietary rules about pork and shellfish, let's stop and ask ourselves when was the last time we had a nice juicy plate of insect larvae or a bowl of worms for dinner? People in other cultures eat such things. Moral: we Americans have just as many dietary taboos as any other culture.

Similarly, when things or people are called "holy" in remote antiquity, the distinction between the ritual and moral implications of this are not worked out too clearly either. What is emphasized is that the person has been ritually set apart by God for a particular purpose. But it does not necessarily follow that the one ritually set apart is a particularly saintly person (the story of Samson in Judges 13-16 is illustrative of this), and it may even be that the one ritually set apart turns out to be a scoundrel. This, for instance, is what governs the odd behavior (by modern standards) of David when he is pursued by the paranoid and murderous King Saul in 1 Samuel. David has a number of chances to kill his persecutor fair and square but refuses to do so. Why? Because, as he puts it, "I would not put forth my hand against the Lord's anointed" (1 Samuel 26:23). The holiness of Saul is due, not to his saintly goodness, but to the fact that he was ritually set apart for the service of God as king, and David feels himself bound to honor that despite Saul's murderous campaign against him.

Eventually, though, the connection of the idea of holiness with that of a heart or spirit set apart for the service of God inexorably wins ground as the Jewish tradition gives birth to the Christian tradition. In Mary, we see an absolute identification of the two. When she gives birth to Jesus, there is no question that she is "set apart" for the most utterly unique task to which God has ever called a mere mortal. But there is also no question in the Catholic tradition that she who was summoned to that task was made utterly worthy to accomplish it in every way. She is "conceived without sin" and is granted the singular gift of being the most saved person who ever lived. She is, in her person, the New Wineskin into whom the New Wine is first poured (cf. Luke 5:36-39).

Mary is ultimately holy for the same reason that every saint is holy: because the Holy Spirit is upon her. The coming of the Holy Spirit upon Mary in the conception of Jesus was not the first time the Spirit had come upon her. Mary was graced with the help of her Son's Spirit long before her Son took flesh in her womb. It was he who preserved her from sin from conception onward. It was his grace that did it, not some goodness of her own that owed nothing to the help of God. Mary was readied by grace to be holy. Her holiness made her open to further grace. This is the pattern of the Christian life. Grace enables us to respond to God, and our response to God opens us to more grace, so we enter by grace into a life of sowing to the Spirit and reaping of the Spirit (Galatians 6:8). Mary herself went from grace to grace, not merely conceiving and bearing the Word Incarnate, but pondering his life in her heart, going with him to the agony of the cross, rejoicing at his resurrection, welcoming his Spirit yet again at Pentecost, and finally following him to heaven in her glorious assumption, becoming the very first person to fully enjoy what we who believe in him will all one day enjoy in the resurrection.

This is why the early Church dubs her *Theotokos* (literally "God-bearer"), or "Mother of God." That title does not mean Catholics think Mary is the creator of God. It does not mean she gave birth to an ordinary man who was "adopted" or temporarily "possessed" by the Logos, or Second Person of the Trinity, becoming two persons, one human and one divine, occupying a single head. Rather, it means Jesus is fully God and fully man, Son of God and son of Mary: one person with two natures, divine and human. Mary did not give birth to some abstraction any more than your mother did. We do not introduce our mothers to our friends, saying, "This is the mother of my human nature." We say, "This is my mother." So did God when he lived in Nazareth with Mary.

Mary gave birth to a person who is God and man. Because she did, we have been saved, since salvation means sharing in Christ's divinized human nature. That is why we honor her and call her "Holy Mary, Mother of God." She was set apart as no other mortal has ever been by the Holy One who chooses the vessels he will honor according to his own purposes. Holy Mary has been more highly honored than any other creature, and it is only fitting that we acknowledge that fact, just as we acknowledge and honor the many other lesser creatures whom God has likewise exalted by his grace.

Chapter 17

PRAY FOR US SINNERS

There's a reason ancient churches such as St. Peter's Basilica in Rome are located where they are. It's not that such places are scenic. It's because a saint or a martyr was buried at that site. Church buildings subsequently were built because the people of God were already meeting there to pray, listen to Scripture, celebrate the sacraments, and ask the saint buried there to pray for them. This was no small part of why the early Christians gave pagans the willies and periodically wound up as martyrs themselves. For Christians usually met at night (since that's when slaves had free time, and many Christians were slaves), in a graveyard, and they were said to eat somebody's body and blood — all while speaking to the dead!

You'd think people would have gotten the general gist of what Catholics are really up to in the following two thousand years, but one of the main things that still gives people the willies is confusion over what is going on when Catholics say to Mary, "Pray for us sinners!"

I can relate to those with the willies. When I got married to my cradle-Catholic wife, I wanted nothing to do with that stuff and begged her to leave off what I took to be the dangerous pagan practice of praying to Mary. As I had been taught to think, prayer to the saints was indistinguishable from séance or summoning the dead and was therefore forbidden by Scripture. As near as I could tell, the whole thing was occultism. Her prayers to Mary and the saints genuinely worried me, particularly since Scripture seemed to plainly condemn it:

> And when they say to you, "Consult the mediums and the wizards who chirp and mutter," should not a people consult

their God? Should they consult the dead on behalf of the living? To the teaching and to the testimony! Surely for this word which they speak there is no dawn. They will pass through the land, greatly distressed and hungry; and when they are hungry, they will be enraged and will curse their king and their God, and turn their faces upward; and they will look to the earth, but behold, distress and darkness, the gloom of anguish; and they will be thrust into thick darkness. (Isaiah 8:19-22)

This wasn't helped by my various encounters with uneducated Catholics who sometimes got fuddled and saw no problem with things like horoscopes and divination. So it seemed obvious to me that the Church had somehow lost track of the Ten Commandments and fallen into a foggy sort of occultism.

Until, that is, I took the time to find out what the Church actually said about both occultism and prayer to the saints. As I discovered, the Church actually was quite aware of the dangers of the occult. For example, the *Catechism* says:

God can reveal the future to his prophets or to other saints. Still, a sound Christian attitude consists in putting oneself confidently into the hands of Providence for whatever concerns the future, and giving up all unhealthy curiosity about it. . . .

All forms of *divination* are to be rejected: recourse to Satan or demons, conjuring up the dead or other practices falsely supposed to "unveil" the future (cf. Deuteronomy 18:10; Jeremiah 29:8). Consulting horoscopes, astrology, palm reading, interpretation of omens and lots, the phenomena of clairvoyance, and recourse to mediums all conceal a desire for power over time, history, and, in the last analysis, other human beings, as well as a wish to conciliate hidden powers. They contradict the honor, respect, and loving fear that we owe to God alone. (CCC 2115-2116, emphasis in original)

That was a surprise to me. Why was the Church teaching us to regard necromancy, divination, horoscopes, and the rest as sins against the First Commandment (". . . You shall not have strange gods before me") if, as I had supposed, they had forgotten the First Commandment? If the Church warns us to avoid the occult, then why does she pray to saints?

The answer of the Church turned out to be straightforward. We pray to saints because they aren't dead, because they aren't replacements for God, and because they remain our brothers and sisters in Christ.

It's like this: there are three states of the Church, but only one Church. The Church exists here on earth, in purgatory, and in heaven. Death does nothing whatever to sever that communion, which is why we can pray for the dead and they can pray for us. As the *Catechism* says:

> **958** *Communion with the dead.* "In full consciousness of this communion of the whole Mystical Body of Jesus Christ, the Church in its pilgrim members, from the very earliest days of the Christian religion, has honored with great respect the memory of the dead; and 'because it is a holy and a wholesome thought to pray for the dead that they may be loosed from their sins' she offers her suffrages for them."[64] Our prayer for them is capable not only of helping them, but also of making their intercession for us effective.
>
> **959** *In the one family of God.* "For if we continue to love one another and to join in praising the Most Holy Trinity — all of us who are sons of God and form one family in Christ — we will be faithful to the deepest vocation of the Church."[65]

This, after all, was at least part of the point of the story of Jesus' reply to the Sadducees, who rejected the notion of the resurrection of the dead and hoped to catch Jesus in his words and show him up for a fool:

The same day Sadducees came to him, who say that there is no resurrection; and they asked him a question, saying, "Teacher, Moses said, 'If a man dies, having no children, his brother must marry the widow, and raise up children for his brother.' Now there were seven brothers among us; the first married, and died, and having no children left his wife to his brother. So too the second and third, down to the seventh. After them all, the woman died. In the resurrection, therefore, to which of the seven will she be wife? For they all had her."

But Jesus answered them, "You are wrong, because you know neither the scriptures nor the power of God. For in the resurrection they neither marry nor are given in marriage, but are like angels in heaven. And as for the resurrection of the dead, have you not read what was said to you by God, 'I am the God of Abraham, and the God of Isaac, and the God of Jacob'? He is not God of the dead, but of the living." (Matthew 22:23-32)

It was also, in part, the point of the story of the Transfiguration, when the extremely dead Moses illustrated Jesus' point above by appearing with Elijah and speaking with Jesus in the hearing of the apostles (Matthew 17:1-8).

Prayer to the saints is sharply distinct from "consulting the dead" precisely because it does not attempt to make an end run around God, nor treat a creature as God, nor acquire from the dead forbidden knowledge or power. The theology behind prayer to the saints is, in fact, straightforward and solidly biblical. It is centered in the Light of the World, of which the "angel of light" is a cheesy imitation. It rests on the thoroughly biblical fact that the blessed dead, connected with us in Christ, are indeed aware of earthly doings (Hebrews 12:1). Scripture promises that those in Christ shall, in glory, "be like him," conformed to his image in every way (1 John 3:2; Romans 8:29). Even on this earth, we are given the glorious task of carrying out his work by praying for one another and exercising spiritual gifts for the building up of the Body of Christ (Romans 12). The Church, believing the reality that we go from one degree of glory to another (2 Corinthians 3:18), has always believed that this glorious participation in the saving work of Christ will be ours in even fuller measure when we enter into heaven. Since we are "members one of another" (Romans 12:5) we can, in Christ and only in Christ, seek the prayers and help of fellow members of the Body, both here and in heaven.

The bottom line is that séances are not the same as prayer to the saints, for the same reason magic is not the same as miracles, and horoscopes are not the same as prophecy. Séances, magic, horoscopes, and divination are parodies of a reality that God offers us, the reality of our connectedness in Christ. In contrast to the teaching of Christ, the obvious goal of the medium or diviner is neither union with God nor communion with "the riches of his glorious inheritance in the saints" (Ephesians 1:18), but becoming "like God, knowing good and evil" (Genesis 3:5).

It is a different thing, therefore, if a person asks a member of the Body of Christ, whether living or dead, to pray for us. It's not idolatry because prayer to a saint is not worship, any more than bowing to an audience or kneeling to propose marriage is. "Pray" is simply an old-fashioned word for "request," as in "I pray thee, do thou get me another ale, sirrah, and I shall reckon it an act of kindness withal." Thus, in asking me to pray for you, you are "praying to" me in the sense the Catholic Church means it. To "pray to" the saints is likewise not to adore them as gods. Rather, it is simply to address them as fellow members of the Body of Christ. This is very significant, for it is to consciously place both oneself and the saint addressed in the Communion of Saints, which is united with the Blessed Trinity and, in the Trinity, with us. In other words, Catholic prayer to the dead fully acknowledges our connectedness entirely within Christ.

This is supremely so with the Queen of the Saints, Mary, because she has been given to us as our Mother by Christ himself. That is why John records the incident at the foot of the cross when Jesus tells Mary, "Behold, your son," and the Beloved Disciple, "Behold, your mother" (John 19:26-27). It is also why John speaks in language that blends Marian imagery into a figure who also recalls the virgin daughter of Zion and the Church — the woman clothed with the sun in Revelation 12 — and tells of the great red dragon that seeks not only to devour her Son but who "went off to make war on the rest of her offspring, on those who keep the commandments of God and bear testimony to Jesus" (Revelation 12:17).

That dragon has a name, according to John. He is "that ancient serpent, who is called the Devil and Satan, the deceiver of the whole world" (Revelation 12:9), and the two figures John sees opposing the dragon are the archangel Michael and the woman. Both act with the power and authority of Jesus Christ. The dragon is defeated, not by mankind's own strength, but by joining in the suffering of Christ crucified:

> And I heard a loud voice in heaven, saying, "Now the salvation and the power and the kingdom of our God and the authority of his Christ have come, for the accuser of our brethren has been thrown down, who accuses them day and night before our God. And they have conquered him by the blood of the Lamb and by the word of their testimony, for they loved not their lives even unto death. (Revelation 12:10-11)

That is why we ask Mary to pray for us — because we are commanded to pray for one another and to ask prayer of one another. Mary, the icon of the Church, does for us what any member of the Church would do; she intercedes for us as Christ commands us to intercede for one another. She does it as a mother because she *is* our Mother, given to us by Jesus Christ himself as his final gift to us from the cross.

It is telling, and beautiful, that the prayer is not merely "pray for us" but "pray for us *sinners*." We come to our Mother in Christ as we come to Christ himself: as sinners and slobs, not as shiny, happy people. There's no question of having to be good enough. We are told to come now, without delay and without combing our hair or washing our faces. To be sure, there will be time and occasion to get washed up (in the sacraments of Baptism and Reconciliation) and, to be sure, seeking Christ means doing what we can to change and conform our lives to him. But first, we come to him through the intercession of Mary and the Church for whom she stands and ask for grace rather than try to earn the love of God and put him in our debt. We simply come — as sinners — and trust that God, in his love and mercy, will receive us. The promise is that he shall. Every single time. No matter what.

Chapter 18

NOW AND AT THE HOUR
OF OUR DEATH

I once read an interview with Garrison Keillor in which he recounted going to a funeral. During the final prayers, the minister prayed for the deceased "and for the next person here who is going to die." He said that most of the guests were outraged and offended, but that he was moved and appreciative. He liked the fact that the Christian tradition does not candy-coat things with promises of perpetual youth and vitality. The fact is, nobody's getting out of here alive. You are going to die, and your body is going to rot and be eaten by worms. Face it.

The Hail Mary faces it. The last prayer we make to the glorious Virgin is eminently practical. It is entirely directed toward "getting our affairs in order." Whether from germ, or steel, or bullet, or thirst, or drowning, or heat, or cold, or cancer, or chemo, or by the hand of man, this jolly round of days we have known since the insolence of our youth is going to be terminated, and every Jack and Jill among us will be left cold and dead. You are dying. You were born that way. Like the vast majority of the human race, you will go down to the grave and vanish forever from the memory of mortal man, utterly forgotten by all mankind. If you don't believe it, tell me one thing you know about your great-great-great-great-grandmother.

But you will not be forgotten by God. The promise of the Gospel is that you are known by him utterly and that, through faith in his Son, Jesus, you will live in the next world so profoundly that your life on this earth will be a mere eye blink compared with the deeps of eternity that await you in the Blessed Trinity. Your death will, in this reckoning, be your birthday, the day you came home to heaven, where you belong.

It is from this perspective that we pray the Hail Mary. We ask the first and most redeemed of Christ's saints to help us enter into all the glory God desires for us in the Risen Christ. In doing so, we approach death pretty much the way Jesus tells us to do it: not by looking to the future so much as by looking at the present in light of eternity, where God is always alive and very present.

That's why Paul tells us, "Behold, now is the acceptable time; behold, now is the day of salvation" (2 Corinthians 6:2). It is also why Jesus says, "Do not be anxious about tomorrow, for tomorrow will be anxious for itself. Let the day's own trouble be sufficient for the day" (Matthew 6:34). One of the corollaries of this is that we should, oddly, be aware of Judgment Day but not anxious about it. That's because Judgment Day is happening right now.

Oh sure, there will be a consummation of all things at the end of time. Oh sure, the billions of souls who have died will stand before the all-conquering and glorious King and receive the mercy and justice of Almighty God, and the whole created order will be transmuted into the unthinkable glory of the New Heaven and the New Earth, and the Lamb shall reign in the New Jerusalem forever and ever, while the damned shall grind their teeth in the outer darkness and the blessed and glorified saints shall enjoy the radiant splendor of the living God for endless ages of ages. But in the meantime, the only way to heaven is through the Sacrament of the Present Moment, presenting our lives to the judgment and guidance of the Holy Spirit on a moment-by-moment basis. Today, now, this very instant, Jesus calls you to receive and live his salvation. This is why the Hail Mary does not merely direct our prayer to the far-off someday. It directs it to this very second, which is the only moment we can do something about. The past is gone. The future is not ours to see, much less control. Only this moment — right now — is yours to choose God. So we ask our heavenly Mother to pray for us sinners *now*.

Indeed, in a certain sense, now *is* the hour of our death. The love of wisdom, said the Greeks, is the practice of death. Our lives are one long rehearsal for it, so that we won't blow our lines and look like idiots before the heavenly audience when the curtain rises on eternity. The angels, saints, and martyrs — the whole cloud of witnesses — are a very attentive and very supportive audience, rooting for us all the way and, like our Lord, celebrating even our stumbles if we do them with a good will (cf. Hebrews 12:1-2) — and none of them more so than our Blessed Mother. Like our Lord, she knows that our death can come upon us suddenly and without warning. In the Hail Mary, God gives us the gracious gift of having said our prayers and made our peace with him beforehand, should we not have the opportunity when we need to.

That's the beauty of rote prayer: it makes us all eloquent far beyond our native ability. This is counterintuitive in our informal age, which imagines that only extemporaneous prayer is "from the heart," and which derides "parrot prayer" as inauthentic. But, in fact, when we store up the prayers of the Church in our souls, they *become* the prayers of the heart. We should know this, since it is precisely how our parents civilized us with the precious gifts of "Please" and "Thank you" and raised us up from being the uncouth grabby ingrates we were before we learned these magic incantations that opened the key to healthy adulthood. In the same way, having words like "Pray for us sinners, now and at the hour of our death" squirreled away in the soul ensures that we will not have to suddenly think them up on our own when we are reeling with shock after the miscarriage, the auto accident, or the notice from the Defense Department regretting to inform us that our world has just been shattered.

For the first — and last — truth about prayer is, to repeat Father Tugwell's profound insight, that we don't know how to do it. As Paul says, "the Spirit helps us in our weakness" (Romans 8:26), particularly by giving us a rich tradition of prayers from the Church that we would never have thought of ourselves in a million years. Even on our good days, our prayers are often inept, but on our own, in crisis situations, we usually go numb or babble incoherently, or spout inanity or simply go to pieces. At such times, we discover that the Cult of the Informal is desperately inadequate to help us find the deepest places of our heart and give them voice. What we need is liturgy, rote prayers, the Rosary, and the grief of God's Son and Sorrowful Mother, crying our bitter tears in the Sorrowful Mysteries and reassuring us of the adamantine truth of the Glorious Mysteries.

Here we discover that where we find what is common to all men and women is where we also find what is most intensely personal — the joys, sorrows, and glories of human existence that are the common patrimony of us all. It is here, in the ordinary public prayers of the Church, and not in some mystic cave of contemplation far from the madding crowd, where we meet again the profound consolation of the Mother of Sorrows, who sits enthroned in heaven, reminding us that she, too, has been through the worst thing in the world and that even that could not defeat the incredible hope of the Risen Christ. And we discover that she freely shares with us the astonishing promise that she shall indeed remember us to her Son at that most inevitable hour of our lives: when we die and are, God willing, born to eternal life.

TWO HEARTS IN ONE

Whole books with titles like *A Treasury of Christian Prayer* attest to the fact that the Church has any number of prayers that it might set before us for our contemplation. Some of them, such as the Prayer of St. Francis, are very popular, and others, like Augustine's prayer to the Ancient of Days, are very ancient indeed. Some of them are easy to memorize and serve well for both individual and communal prayer. Some of them, such as the Serenity Prayer or the Prayer of Jabez, enjoy brief popularity and could be capitalized on by a spiritual "marketing campaign," should the Church choose to do so. (Thank God the Church is abysmal at, and has no interest in, "marketing.") Many prayers come from the inspired word of God itself, such as those composed or recorded by Paul and John, or the mighty prayers of praise and adoration found in the Psalms or the book of Revelation. Some prayers come from the pens of the most eloquent and profound saints who ever lived. Others, such as the *Tantum Ergo* or the *Pange Lingua*, have long been associated with the adoration of Jesus in the Holy Eucharist and therefore lie very close to what the Church calls the "source and summit" of the Catholic faith. Still others, such as the *Memorare* or the *Hail, Holy Queen*, collect the Church's Marian devotion into beautiful words of petition that have moved the souls of millions down the years.

Yet, for all that, the Holy Spirit has guided the Church to focus on two prayers — the Our Father and the Hail Mary — as the twin pillars of liturgical worship and popular piety. It is the Spirit speaking through the whole Body of Christ that, in the end, calls to us and speaks through us by these two prayers in particular.

So why these two? The answer, I believe, is in the mystical union of Trinitarian love.

In his great High Priestly Prayer, offered just a few hours before his arrest and crucifixion, Jesus offers a prayer for his Church that is as profound as it is mysterious and impenetrable. He prays:

> "I do not pray for these only, but also for those who believe in me through their word, that they may all be one; even as thou, Father, art in me, and I in thee, that they also may be in us, so that the world may believe that thou hast sent me. The glory which thou hast given me I have given to them, that they may be one even as we are one, I in them and thou in me, that they may become perfectly one, so that the world may know that thou hast sent me and hast loved them even as thou hast loved me." (John 17:20-23)

I make no claim to be able to understand very well this dense mystical language. It strains at the limits of human speech to get across the strange nature of our relationship with God in Christ. How Christ is "in" the Father and the Father is "in" him, and he is "in" us and we are "in" him, is beyond my ken. However, I do think that though I cannot understand it or describe it very well, there are times we begin to experience a little taste of it, even in our human relationships.

Consider, for instance, the curious way in which even our ordinary human relationships sometimes are made richer by the love of a friend for somebody else. I have known and loved people whom I never would have noticed had they not been loved deeply by somebody to whom I was close. Suddenly, through your friend Susan's eyes and "in" her heart, you start to see her friend Joe, and you begin to appreciate what Susan appreciates about him. This is particularly true when your friend Susan falls in love. Her soul doth magnify her lover, and her spirit exults in Joe her boyfriend. You start to appreciate how Joe loves her back. She is in his heart, and he in hers. The whole is greater than the sum of its parts. This is the essence of *eros*, romantic love. And although it is possible that my friend Susan will teach me to appreciate Joe in a way I had not before, it is absolutely forbidden that I, as their friend, should love Susan or Joe in the way that they love each other. The love the Greeks called *eros* makes Lover and Beloved a closed set.

But with *phileo*, or friendship, it's different: there we have a case of the more, the merrier. This is not to be sneezed at as something inferior to *eros*. It was, after all, a band of *friends* whom our Lord sent out to bring the world to faith in Christ. Their *phileo* love for one another was the fuel for kindling the deepest fire of all: the *agape* love of God in the hearts of one another and of their first converts.

Here, too, the whole was greater than the sum of its parts, particularly when the apostles met in council to seek the mind of the Spirit. For, as Jesus promised (John 16:13), the Spirit showed up and continued to lead them into all truth as he spoke from the midst of the love in which Christ had placed them: the love of the Blessed Trinity, in which the Father is in the Son, the Son is in the Father, the Blessed Trinity is in the Church, and the Church is in the Trinity. That's why the Church could dare to say, "It has seemed good to the Holy Spirit *and to us* . . ." (Acts 15:28, emphasis added).

So this curious interpenetration of love — the Beloved in the Lover and the Lover in the Beloved, the Friend in the Circle of Friends — is seen in the lower forms of love such as *eros* and *phileo*, but it reaches its zenith in *agape*, the love who is God. The place *agape* finds its welcome in this world is in the heart and womb of the Blessed Virgin Mary, who is, as St. Ambrose points out, the type of the Church. Where, in our own small ways, we glimpse it in Joe and Susan and the way they look at each other, or in the curious way that a group of friends is somehow more than can be accounted for by each member alone, we see something different, something properly transcendent and supernatural in the utterly unique relationship between Mary and her Son, the God-man. Human language can only gesticulate and point. Every attempt at a metaphor or figure of speech only reveals that human language is inadequate to the task.

So, though Tradition makes use of imagery from *eros* to speak of Christ the Last Adam and Mary the New Eve, or Christ the Bridegroom and his Bride the Church, it is also ringed round with massive artillery to make clear that the language of marriage used to describe the relationship of Christ the Bridegroom and his Bride the Church is *only* an image and not the reality. Christianity never devolves into a sex cult, in which copulation becomes the central rite of union with the deity (as paganism so often did), because Christianity starkly forbids us from mistaking the mere image of heavenly ecstasy that is sex for the reality who is God. Sex, while sacramental, is enshrined in the privacy of the bridal chamber after the sacrament of Marriage. It is not made the central focus of the Mass or performed on the altar in debauched fertility rites, as was common in the paganism of Jesus' own time. For the same reason, the virginity of Christ and Mary is emphasized at every turn, and their utter holiness and purity mark Christianity off from a Dionysian cult from the very start. Indeed, the approach of the Church strikes the perceptive balance. Marriage is a great good (it is a sacrament, after all), but virginity is even better. It is better precisely because it is an image of eschatological fulfillment when earthly good is swallowed up in heavenly ecstasy and "in the resurrection they neither marry nor are given in marriage, but are like angels in heaven" (Matthew 22:30).

Likewise, the language of friendship is sometimes used to describe our relationship with Christ. Jesus himself tells us, "No longer do I call you servants, for the servant does not know what his master is doing; but I have called you friends, for all that I have heard from my Father I have made known to you" (John 15:15). And so, by an astonishing gift of grace, we are granted a curious sort of equality with God (for that is what friendship implies). Yet we cannot presume upon that friendship, nor mistake our relationship with Christ for merely earthly forms of *phileo* any more than we can regard Jesus as a mere mortal bridegroom. He is our friend, and we are his. But we are not buddies, chums, or homies. The imagery of friendship, like the imagery of *eros*, is not to be confused with the reality of the *Agape*, who is God.

In all this, the Our Father and the Hail Mary keep us on an even keel and remind us that at the heart of the faith is the *heart* or, more precisely, the two hearts of God and his Bride. Jesus, of course, has a heart that beats as one with the Father's heart. Indeed, he *is* the heart of the Father. Jesus' humanity is at one with the Father, God in him and he in the Father; but though the focal point of Christian faith is the heart of God revealed in Christ Jesus, it is not the totality, just as the totality of a wheel cannot be the hub alone.

What I mean is this: Christianity is about salvation. Jesus' very name *means* "The Lord is Salvation." But though the heart of God is Jesus, Jesus is not the one being saved. We are. So our hearts must enter into the picture as well. Our hearts must be in Jesus' heart, and he in ours. That is why the Hail Mary is constantly paired with the Our Father in the Church's devotional life, especially in the Rosary.

It is not enough that Jesus triumphed over death and ascended to heaven. If nobody goes with him, the whole exercise was a pointless waste of time. In the Hail Mary, we are perpetually reminded that the human heart Jesus took with him to heaven bore within it the heart of the human being who loved him more than anybody else — and that she followed her heart all the way to heaven. We are given the glad news that we can do the same, as many already have, if we but place our heart in theirs and join in their love for each other. In Jesus, who is the Heart of the Father, and Mary, who gave Jesus both his human heart and her own heart as well, we find our salvation.

NOTES

1. For a thorough and accessible overview of the concept of God's covenant relationship with us, see Dr. Scott Hahn's *A Father Who Keeps His Promises: God's Covenant Love in Scripture* (Ann Arbor, MI: Servant, 1998).

2. Cited in "The Rosary" entry in the *Catholic Encyclopedia* (1913). Available online at http://www.newadvent.org/cathen/13184b.htm, as of March 3, 2011.

3. Ambrose, *Expos. Lc.* II, 7: PL 15, 1555.

4. Robert Farrar Capon, *The Supper of the Lamb: A Culinary Reflection* (Garden City, NY: Doubleday, 1978), p. 85.

5. C. S. Lewis, *Mere Christianity* (New York: Macmillan, 1984), p. 161.

6. J. R .R. Tolkien, "On Fairy-Stories" in *Essays Presented to Charles Williams,* edited by C. S. Lewis (Grand Rapids, MI: Eerdmans, 1966), pp. 82-84.

7. C. S. Lewis, *The Pilgrim's Regress: An Allegorical Apology for Christianity, Reason, and Romanticism* (Grand Rapids, MI: Eerdmans, 1992), p. 204.

8. C. S. Lewis, *The Problem of Pain* (New York: Macmillan, 1976), pp. 145-147.

9. C. S. Lewis, *Mere Christianity* (New York: Macmillan, 1984), p. 120, emphasis added.

10. Augustine of Hippo, *Confessions*, Book I, Chapter 1. Available online at http://www.leaderu.com/cyber/books/augconfessions/bk1.html, as of March 3, 2011.

11. C. S. Lewis, *The Screwtape Letters* (New York: Macmillan, 1970), pp. 12-13.

12. If that reference is opaque to you, then it's long past time you read C. S. Lewis' *The Chronicles of Narnia* (New York: HarperCollins, 1994), with special attention to *The Horse and His Boy* and *The Last Battle.*

13. Søren Kierkegaard, *Purity of Heart Is to Will One Thing* (New York: HarperOne, 1956).

14. Dante Alighieri, *The Divine Comedy: Paradiso*, Canto III, Line 85, from *The Divine Comedy*, translated by Dorothy L. Sayers and Barbara Reynolds (London: Penguin Classics, 2004).

15. Augustine of Hippo, *Homily 7 on the First Epistle of John*, 8. Available online at http://www.newadvent.org/fathers/170207.htm, as of March 4, 2011.

16. Henri Frankfort, Mrs. H. A. Frankfort, John A. Wilson, Thorkild Jacobsen, *Before Philosophy: The Intellectual Adventure of Ancient Man* (London: Penguin, 1946).

17. Michel Barnouin, *"Remarques sur les tableaux numériques du Livre des Nombres,"* RB 76 (1969), pp. 351-364. Michel Barnouin, *"Les recensements du Livre des Nombres et l'astronomie babylonienne,"* VT 27 (1977), pp. 280-303.

18. For a full discussion of John's use of zodiac imagery, see Austin Marsden Farrer, *A Rebirth of Images: The Making of St. John's Apocalypse* (Albany, NY: State University of New York Press, 1986). Also see David Chilton, *The Days of Vengeance: An Exposition of the Book of Revelation* (Fort Worth, TX: Dominion, 1990), pp. 158-159.

19. For a fuller discussion of the relationship between cosmos and temple, see Joshua Berman, *The Temple: Its Meaning and Symbolism Then and Now* (Northvale, NJ: Jason Aronson, 1995), pp. 10-14.

20. Augustine of Hippo, *De sermone Domini in monte* in *Patrologia Latina*, 2, 6, 24: PL 34, 1279.

21. G. K. Chesterton, *Autobiography* (Kent, England: Fisher Press, 1992), p. 340.

22. Cf. John Paul II, *Dives in Misericordia*, 14. Available online at http://www.vatican.va/holy_father/john_paul_ii/encyclicals/documents/hf_jp-ii_enc_30111980_dives-in-misericordia_en.html, as of April 26, 2011.

23. George MacDonald, *Donal Grant,* Chapter 46. Available online at http://www.classicreader.com/read.php/sid./bookid.1206/sec.46, as of March 5, 2011.

24. C. S. Lewis, *The Great Divorce* (New York: HarperOne, 2001), p. 28.

25. Augustine of Hippo, *Confessions*, Book VIII, Chapter 7. Available online at http://www.leaderu.com/cyber/books/augconfessions/bk8.html, as of March 3, 2011.

26. Origen, *De orat.* 29: PG 11, 544CD.

27. Council of Trent (1546): DS 1515.

28. Available online at http://richarddawkins.net/articles/4484, as of March 5, 2011.

29. William Shakespeare, *Hamlet*, Act I, Scene V.

30. G. K. Chesterton, *Orthodoxy* (San Francisco: Ignatius, 1995), pp. 157-158.

31. *Roman Missal*, Eucharistic Prayer IV, 125.

32. Lewis, *The Great Divorce*, p. 80.

33. William Shakespeare, *Henry IV*, Part 1, Act 3, Scene 1.

34. G. K. Chesterton, *The Everlasting Man* (San Francisco: Ignatius, 1993). Also available online at http://www.wikilivres.info/wiki/The_Everlasting_Man, as of September 16, 2011.

35. Heinrich Himmler, Poznan Speech to the SS, October 4, 1943, available online at http://www.holocaust-history.org/himmler-poznan/speech-text.shtml, as of September 17, 2011.

36. Martin Luther, *A Mighty Fortress Is Our God*.

37. *Roman Missal*, Embolism after the Lord's Prayer, 126.

38. Simone de Beauvoir, *The Second Sex* (New York: Vintage, 1989), p. 171.

39. Father Alessio Parente, *Send Me Your Guardian Angel* (Barto, PA: National Centre for Padre Pio, 1984), p. 65.

40. Liturgy of St. John Chrysostom.

41. Proclus, *Laudatio in S. Dei Gen. ort.*, I, 3.

42. Hippolytus, *Against Beron and Helix*, Frag VIII.

43. Ibid.

44. Hippolytus, *A Discourse on the End of the World*.

45. Origen, *Homily 1*.

46. Ambrose, *Commentary on Psalm 118*, 22-30.

47. Theodorus of Jerusalem in Mansi, XII, 1140.

48. Ephraem the Syrian, *Precationes ad Deiparam* in Opp. Graec. Lat., III, 524-37.

49. G. K. Chesterton, *Gloria in Profundis* (London: Faber & Gwyer, 1928). Also available online at http://en.wikisource.org/wiki/Gloria_in_Profundis, as of September 17, 2011.

50. For a good argument that Isaiah's prophecy is immediately fulfilled by the birth of Hezekiah, see Rev. William G. Most, "The Problem

of Isaiah 7:14," *Faith and Reason*, Summer 1992, available online at http://www.ewtn.com/library/SCRIPTUR/FR92203.TXT as of March 5, 2011.

51. For a fine attempt to grapple with the question of why evangelicals have such an instinctive distrust of Marian devotion, see "The Blessed Evangelical Mary," by Timothy George, in *Christianity Today*, December 2003, available online at http://www.christianitytoday.com/ct/2003/december/1.34.html, as of March 5, 2011.

52. Father Joseph Mohr.

53. George Weigel, *Witness to Hope* (New York: HarperCollins, 2005), p. 577.

54. Available online at http://www.biblefortoday.org/PDF/33_Errors_of_Rome.pdf, as of March 8, 2011.

55. Available online at http://www.holybiblesays.org/articles.php?ID=199, as of March 8, 2011.

56. Available online at http://www.reachingcatholics.org/hailmarymd.html, as of March 8, 2011.

57. Available online at http://new.carmforums.org/dc/dcboard.php?az=show_mesg&forum=107&topic_id=213665&mesg_id=213686&page=, as of May 2, 2008.

58. Available online at http://www.biblebelievers.org.au/radio006.htm, as of March 8, 2011.

59. Available online at http://www.evalverdeministries.org/The_Humanity_of_the_Lord_Jesus.htm, as of May 2, 2008.

60. Available online at http://christianbookshelf.org/mcgarvey/the_four-fold_gospel/xxii_jesus_works_his_first.htm, as of March 8, 2011.

61. Available online at http://www.waysidechurch.org/mark/mark11.htm, as of March 8, 2011.

62. G. K. Chesterton, "The Macbeths" in *The Spice of Life*, available online at http://wikilivres.info/wiki/The_Spice_of_Life_and_Other_Essays/The_Macbeths, as of March 8, 2011.

63. The text of the *Gloria* is available online at http://old.usccb.org/romanmissal/, as of February 2, 2012. English translation of the *Gloria* is by the International Consultation on English Texts (ICET).

64. *Lumen Gentium*, 50; cf. 2 Maccabees 12:45.

65. *Lumen Gentium*, 51; cf. Hebrews 3:6.

SELECTED BIBLIOGRAPHY

Augustine of Hippo, *Confessions*, Book I, Chapter 1. Available online at http://www.leaderu.com/cyber/books/augconfessions/bk1.html, as of March 3, 2011.

————, *Homily 7 on the First Epistle of John*, 8. Available online at http://www.newadvent.org/fathers/170207.htm, as of March 4, 2011.

————, *De sermone Domini in monte* in *Patrologia Latina*, edited by J. P. Migne (Paris: 1841-1855).

Beauvoir, Simone de, *The Second Sex* (New York: Vintage, 1989).

Capon, Robert Farrar, *The Supper of the Lamb: A Culinary Reflection* (Garden City, NY: Doubleday, 1978).

Catechism of the Catholic Church. Available online at http://www.scborromeo.org/ccc.htm, as of March 4, 2011.

Catholic Encyclopedia (1913), "The Rosary." Available online at http://www.newadvent.org/cathen/13184b.htm, as of March 3, 2011.

Chesterton, G. K., *Autobiography* (Kent, England: Fisher Press, 1992).

————, *The Everlasting Man* (San Francisco: Ignatius, 1993). Also available online at http://www.wikilivres.info/wiki/The_Everlasting_Man, as of September 16, 2011.

————, *Gloria in Profundis* (London: Faber & Gwyer, 1928). Also available online at http://en.wikisource.org/wiki/Gloria_in_Profundis, as of September 17, 2011.

————, *Orthodoxy* (San Francisco: Ignatius, 1995).

————, "The Macbeths" in *The Spice of Life*. Available online at http://wikilivres.info/wiki/The_Spice_of_Life_and_Other_Essays/The_Macbeths, as of March 8, 2011.

Dante Alighieri, *The Divine Comedy*, translated by Dorothy L. Sayers and Barbara Reynolds (London: Penguin Classics, 2004).

Frankfort, Henri, Mrs. H. A. Frankfort, John A. Wilson, and Thorkild Jacobsen, *Before Philosophy: The Intellectual Adventure of Ancient Man* (London: Penguin, 1946).

Hahn, Scott, *A Father Who Keeps His Promises: God's Covenant Love in Scripture* (Ann Arbor, MI: Servant, 1998).

John Paul II, *Dives in Misericordia*. Available online at http://www .vatican.va/holy_father/john_paul_ii/encyclicals/documents/ hf_jp-ii_enc_30111980_dives-in-misericordia_en.html, as of April 26, 2011.

Kierkegaard, Søren, *Purity of Heart Is to Will One Thing* (New York: HarperOne, 1956).

Lewis, C. S., *The Great Divorce* (New York: HarperOne, 2001).

———, *Mere Christianity* (New York: Macmillan, 1984).

———, *The Pilgrim's Regress: An Allegorical Apology for Christianity, Reason, and Romanticism* (Grand Rapids, MI: Eerdmans, 1992).

———, *The Problem of Pain* (New York: Macmillan, 1976).

———, *The Screwtape Letters* (New York: Macmillan, 1970).

MacDonald, George, *Donal Grant,* Chapter 46. Available online at http://www.classicreader.com/read.php/sid./bookid.1206/sec.46, as of March 5, 2011.

Origen, *De oratione* in *Patrologia Graeca*, edited by J. P. Migne (Paris: 1857-1866).

Parente, Father Alessio, *Send Me Your Guardian Angel* (Barto, PA: National Centre for Padre Pio, 1984).

Thérèse of Lisieux, St., *The Final Conversations*, translated by John Clarke (Washington, DC: ICS, 1977).

Tolkien, J. R. R., "On Fairy-Stories" in *Essays Presented to Charles Williams,* edited by C. S. Lewis (Grand Rapids, MI: Eerdmans, 1966).

Tugwell, Father Simon, *Prayer in Practice* (Springfield, IL: Templegate, 1974).

Weigel, George, *Witness to Hope* (New York: HarperCollins, 2005).

MARK P. SHEA is a popular author of books on the beauty and truth of the Catholic faith, including *By What Authority?* and *The Work of Mercy.* He is an award-winning columnist for the *National Catholic Register*, a frequent contributor to *Our Sunday Visitor*, an internationally known speaker, an avid blogger, a frequent guest on radio and TV, and an occasional actor in film. He lives in Seattle.